Day Trading Beginner Guide + Options:

Trading Strategies to Make Money Online in Cryptocurrency, Forex,Penny Market, Stocks and Futures.Learn Trading Psychology,Money Management & Discipline Tactics.

Table Of Contents

before attempting any techniques outlined in this book.

By reading this document, the reader agrees that under no circumstances is the author responsible for any losses, direct or indirect, which are incurred as a result of the use of information contained within this document, including, but not limited to, — errors, omissions, or inaccuracies.

Disclaimer

While the author has exerted the best efforts during the course of preparing and finishing this book, he makes no warranties or representations regarding the accuracy or completeness of the contents of this book. He specifically disclaims any implied warranties of merchantability or fitness for a particular purpose.

The discussions, strategies, and tips given in this book may be not be suitable for your situation. Therefore, it is best to consult accordingly with a professional as needed. The author shall not be held liable for any loss of profit or damages, including but not limited to special, incidental, or consequential damages.

Introduction

Trading used to be the focus of many corporate and institutional entities, with direct access to closed trading systems. However, the recent technological advances and the boom of the World Wide Web have leveled the walls covering their playing field.

Now, trading, specifically day-trading, is available to everyone, even to you. With the right tools and knowledge, you can capitalize on market crashes. Many are afraid of bubbles and corrections, but after you're done with this book, you can upgrade your standard of living and take advantage of any economic trend.

Today, the markets for stocks, domestic currencies, and other securities are much more accessible than they used to be 20 years ago. Volatility is their key characteristic. Hence, beginners will find it hard to win in zero-sum markets. That's why you need genuine trading skills to generate profit by buying and selling financial instruments. After the 2000 stock market crash, many traders, especially beginners, lost a lot of money.

That's the danger of knowing little in this field. You can lose your hard-winnings and your capital in just one moment. If you're too aggressive, you can even lose everything in your life. But, if you make it big, you can be crazily rich!

You can generate money in your own home, while wearing pajamas, sipping a cup of coffee, and slouching on your sofa. You can be your own boss, with just your pets, serving as your workmate and supervisor.

When you acquire the skills of successful and seasoned day-traders, you can build real wealth and diversify your financial portfolio. So, even if another blanket of a Great Depression covers the world, your money basket won't run out of funds for you and your loved ones.

Containing the essentials and the secrets of day trading, this book will give you the push you need to start in the field. Featuring the rare trading topics below, "Day Trading Options" can definitely make you an instant day trader!

> Risk management and money management for your capital and future trades

> Comprehensive guides to fundamental and technical analysis

> Beginner to advanced day trading tips, strategies, and lessons

> Learn trading psychology and be able to read market behavior

> Gain the skill to develop your own trading system

> Be acquainted with the indicators that can help you come up with profitable predictions

Thanks for downloading this book, I hope you enjoy the journey.

Disclaimer

The data and lessons provided in this book are solely for informational purposes. All information provided by "Day Trading Options" is considered in good faith. However, we have no liability, under any circumstance, to any damage or loss incurred by the reader.

Step 1: Learn How to Trade

Eight years after the first-ever stock market crash of the 21st century, those who came back to the market ran again. They sought safety, trying to take what's left of their wealth. They tried to find ways to manage their portfolio--or the remainder of it. Since the Great Depression, 2008 was considered the worst year for stocks, Forex, and securities trading.

The convention of buying and holding died after the first crash. With the second, traders started looking for ways to trade and invest. Although some still practice meticulous portfolio balancing, with a type of buy and hold strategy, they scrutinized and modified their holdings after the crash. Others successfully got out, completely, but what happened to those who weren't able to? They lost their capital.

Before you try facing the market every morning, why not learn the fundamentals of day trading first. You can't trade efficiently if you've no idea of what close and open positions are? Are they similar to position trading? You must learn the answers to such questions before you actually start trading your money for success.

The Goal of Day Traders

Trading is the act of buying and selling securities (e.g., futures, options, and swaps) based on short-term movement. The goal of day trading is to gain profit from "price movements." When the price of a stock has increased by 10%, then the people who have purchased shares of that stock can make a profit. Active trading, like day-trading, aims to capture market trends and make profits from such events.

The goal of active trading is to "beat the market" through timing and identification of profitable trades. Most times, day-traders resell their stocks hours after they've purchased them. Within day-trading, there are numerous trading strategies that you can employ.

Perhaps, day-trading is the most popular trading style next to position trading. Others consider this style as a methodology since it's a form of speculation in securities. As its name implies, it's the method of buying and selling securities within the day.

Position traders, in contrast to day traders, holds a position in security for a long period. The position could be held for weeks, months, or even years. This is considered the longest holding period among all active trading styles. Position trading greatly considers the long-term performance of an asset.

For example, Company X (a telco company) will officially launch in 2024. The odds, which involve the indicators for the price movement of X's stocks and assets, are in favor of Company X. This implies that, in the long term, the value of Company X and its assets will likely rise before 2024.

Day traders, on the other hand, focuses on the short-term benefits and price movements of financial assets, like currencies, stocks, and options.

Conventionally, professional day-traders are the ones who invest heavily in day trading. Specialists and market makers are what you can call trading experts. However, throughout the years, electronic trading has continuously chipped and destroyed the walls around the playing fields of banks, billionaires, and financial institutions.

Many have now made "trading" as their primary source of income. For such people, it's a medium that allowed them to diversify their portfolio, whether by engaging in active trading or offering their technical know-how and services to others.

Many ply their skills in the international markets. Those who like thrills take risks and treat day trading as a full-time job or a business venture. Day-traders, in particular, don't stay in a position overnight. They resell stocks and securities hours after they've purchased them or the day after that. Swing traders, on the other hand, eye opportunities months after the actual purchase. In other words, they hoard securities in the hopes of making huge profits in the future.

This book will be focusing more on day trading, but by the time you're done reading this, you will have the confidence to enter any trading market and engage in any type of online transaction or investment.

This book aims to introduce the world of Forex, futures, options, stocks, and cryptocurrencies, as well as the different trading styles. Although it will be focusing on day-trading, reading this is a great starting point to jump-start your career in any type of electronic trading venture.

Enter Day-Trading!

Day-trading can be a crazy business. Traders, investors, and financial analysts work in front of their personal computer, as they react to blips and patterns. Each blip represents a specific amount of real dollars. Their quick decisions enable them to make real cash by the day, unlike salary people, who only get paid once or twice per month.

Another perk of day trading is its versatility. You can trade any tradable security. In fact, you can day trade two or more securities. What's more, you can take very short positions, while investing or swing trading.

Please recall the example in the previous section. Company X has the potential to grow massively in the next four years. The value of its stocks fluctuates every day. This means it's a good security to day-trade! In chapter 3: A Primer to Fundamental Analysis, you'll learn how to choose the securities that could make you rich. Investing in a dead security won't get you anywhere.

Day-trading can bring in quick profits and quick cash. Some platforms allow for the withdrawal of at least 20 USD. Brokerage platforms, like eToro and IQoption, allow for just a $100 deposit. They also offer a $500 free demo account.

When you reach chapter 4: Understanding Technical Analysis, you'll gain insights in choosing the perfect broker for your style and budget. You can use a demo account to practice or test your trading strategy. Chapter 3, 4, and 5 can help you devise a trading system and strategy.

The Golden Rules

Day trading is all about timing, analysis, vigilance, and patience. Does that sound too hard? There are indeed many principles and strategies you can use, but here are some cheats, which are also considered golden rules in the industry:

> ➢ The larger your capital is, the larger your profit will be. Nevertheless, the ability of day traders to generate large sums depends on their skills in making small profits.

> ➢ Tim Sykes, Warren Buffet, and other wealthy traders take close positions in futures, options, and stock markets.

> ➢ Closing positions every day lowers trading risks: market, country, currency, and interest rate risks. These will be further discussed in chapter 4.

> ➢ Don't force your style on stocks that won't make a profit. If you become hasty, you can lose money. In day trading, there are days when nothing seems good to buy, and every trade could be a step closer to bankruptcy.

> ➤ Whenever you're day trading, you have to work fast and be vigilant and patient.

As an individual trader, you face against brokers, financial institutions, central banks, and frequency algorithms that could turn the tides to their favor at any given time. Brokerage firms operate frequency algorithms.

They hedge funds objectively, and they can come up with predictions in seconds they have devoured the necessary data. In less than a blink of your eye, they can make trades. You're up against that, so you gotta be the best version of your trader self, once you're on the actual playing field.

Beginner day traders possess more advantages than human-generated algorithms and large organizations. Why is this so? You can find the answer after you can actually start practicing and executing "mock" trades. This will be possible after you finish chapter 5.

Why Day Trade?

Making a lot of money is the major reason why many people enter the world of trading, of course. Another is improving potential profits from digital transactions. For those who want to grow their portfolio fast, online investing is a way of life. Trading can bring in money for savings and daily expenses.

Regardless of whether you invest through stocks or Forex, a portfolio with securities can give you superior returns. But this will only happen if you're willing to work at it. Those who decide to take the extra mile--to learn anything and everything about trading--do more than just ride the tide of the most recent economic trend. They can also search for loopholes and opportunities during the "best times" and the "bad times."

When there's a big bubble that's about to pop or there's a great demand for a specific stock, you must find the best places to be in the market. Your decisions should be based on market cycles and economic conditions. The last chapter of this book "Day Trading Futures, Options, and Cryptocurrencies" is all about getting ahead of other traders. In day trading, the benefit of one opportunity is only limited to one individual or entity.

Those people who take the initiative or make the conscious decision to improve their profit potential--the potential of an account, asset, or product to generate revenue--are the ones who become seasoned and successful traders.

Take Warren Buffet and Paul Tudor Jones as examples. They started small, but look at them now. They're two of world's richest! As of January 2021, Warren is the 3rd richest man in the world while Jones ranked 343rd. These are all according to Forbes, a well-refuted American business magazine owned by the Forbes family and the Integrated Whale Media Investments.

They, along with the other world-renowned traders, watch markets like vultures. They can create an opportunity for profits even when there's an impending recession. They had watched technical signals before the 2000 stock market crash moved into cash positions. After the stocks tumbled, they carefully humped back in the market once the opportunities were evident.

What did they do? While they were waiting, they carefully researched trends and watched indicators. They added new stocks to their watch list and removed those that couldn't rise again. The technical signals from charts told them when to close and open positions, or when to get in and get out.

The Difference Between Short and Long Trades

It's now time to get acquainted with some of the terms and technicalities of day trading. Let's start with the two types of trades.

In stock trading, short and long refers to the first action of the trader. Did he buy first or sell first? Long trades takes place when a market participant purchases shares of an asset with the intention to involve in repurchasing in the future. This is also called hedging or investing. Most swing traders do this. They invest in a low-priced asset today because its value will likely increase at a certain point in the future.

On the other hand, selling initiates a short trade. Investors sell their stocks for short trading. Eventually, when the asset reaches its ceiling price, its value will go down. In this case, the investor will then repurchase the asset at a lower price.

That is one-way high-stakes and experienced traders manipulate the market. They make huge profits by selling high. The high price will then attract many fellow traders. This decreases the price of the asset. When the price is lower than the previous noted value, they engage in bulk repurchasing.

A short trade, on the one hand, takes place when you sell first. Short traders often repurchase the same stock at a lower price.

When you're "going long," this means you've purchased a security and you're waiting so that you can sell the asset when its price increases. Day traders use the words "long" and "buy" interchangeably. So, please don't be confused about this.

Some apps and web-based brokerage platforms feature entry buttons marked "buy" or "long." Often, the terms are utilized to describe open positions, like "I'm long Sony." This indicates that you own a specific amount of public shares of Sony--the Japanese electronics giant.

-Long Trading Potential

Day traders like to say "go long" or "going long" to show interest in making a purchase for a specific asset. For example, by taking a long position on 100 shares of stock XYX at $5 per unit, the transaction cost will be $5,000. This implies that you bought 100 units of Stock XYX at $5,000.

Hence, if you sell all of those shares at $5,200, you're taking a short position because you're actually selling your shares. If there's an opposing trade and you're able to sell those units, then your net profit will be $200.

By going long, the potential for profit is limitless. Why is this so? The selling value of a popular asset can increase continuously. Then, if you invest in one hundred shares of a stock at $2, its value can go up to $10, $12, or $15 over a certain period.

The negative side of price increase is a reversal--a sudden gradual or instant price decrease. For example, if you offer your stocks at $10.90 per share, you'll receive $10,900 on your $11,000 trade. In this case, you lose a hundred dollars plus the transaction fee. The largest possible loss in the given situation can occur if the price per share becomes $0.0. This results in a $1 loss per share. Day trading can minimize and prevent such huge losses.

-Short Trades

Taking short positions can be intimidating to most beginner traders. In reality, they need to buy something for them to make a profit. When going short (taking a short position), day traders sell securities before purchasing them.

They do this in the hopes of making a profit from a price decrease. Their trade will only generate profits if the amount they borrowed is lower compared to the selling price of the asset.

Traders utilize the words "short" and "sell" interchangeably. Likewise, some apps and trading platforms feature clickable buttons marked "sell" or "short." The use of the word "short" in the sentence "I'm going short Apple" indicates that you're offering Apple stock.

Day traders who like taking short positions often say "go short" or "going short." This indicates that they're interested in taking a short position in a specific asset. For example, if you take a short position on 500 shares of YYY stock at $9.0, you will receive $4,500 in your account. Your trading account will have -500 shares. In the future, you've to bring the balance to zero by purchasing at least 500 shares of that same stock. Unless you do this, you won't know the odds and the loss or profit of the position you're in.

The Major Markets Available in Electronic Trading

-Forex

In foreign exchanges (Forex markets), the spot exchange FX rate is the current rate of exchange of a currency pair. The market determines the rate of every currency being traded in the exchange. As well, all aspects of trading and converting currencies are determined at current (spot) prices.

The major participants in this exchange are international banks and large financial centers. Day and night, except for Saturdays and Sundays, these financial organizations serve as mediums of exchange for millions of traders.

Also known as the currency market, the Forex market is the largest market in the world. It's also the most liquid and has accounted for billions of trades per day. In 2010, it has accounted for $3 trillion of daily trading. Although it hasn't existed a century ago, it's where the majority of day-traders buy and sell securities.

The Foreign Exchange market facilitates the trades of one currency for another. Even though daily currency trades can be also conducted electronically, like stock trading, the two markets are quite different. Currencies are traded in pairs, while stocks are traded in units.

-The Options Market

The options market is a marketplace that enables participants to take positions in the derivative of an asset\security. Hence, the option--a contract that enables an investor to trade a financial instrument like an index or ETF at a set price over a certain period--is based on specific securities. The value of options and other inputs changes with the value or the lack of that the asset in question provides.

-CFDs

CFD stands for Contract for Difference. This is an arrangement made in derivatives trades, wherein the differences in the given settlement between the first and last trade prices are settled by cash. The settlement leads to a cash payment, rather than settling in bonds, stocks, or commodities.

A settlement, in finance and trading, is a business process, by which securities or interests in securities are physically delivered to fulfill contractual obligations. These days, settlements typically take place in central securities depositories (CSDs).

A CSD is a financial organization that holds securities like shares or stocks in dematerialized or certificated form. With this, ownership can be transferred through a book entry. This allows brokers, electronic platforms, and financial organizations to hold securities at a single location. This makes them available for electronic clearing and settlement--a fast and efficient way.

The Market Conditions

You've just been acquainted with the major markets in electronic trading. It's now time to talk about the market conditions. Keep in mind that they aren't actual marketplaces. Rather, they're like trends that you can use in Forex trading and technical analysis.

-What's a Bull Market?

A bull market isn't actually a type of market, but it's considered as a factor or condition that affects exchanges. In any exchange/market, there are two types of trends. It's either prices are increasing or decreasing. A bull market is like a bull using its horns in an upward motion. Rising prices characterize a bull market.

When market prices are high or an asset's price increases by over 20%, the condition is referred to as a bull market. Usually, a bull market occurs when many traders are optimistic over a particular asset or security.

As mentioned earlier, investors with large investments can manipulate market trends. A bull market can arise when many traders and investors are purchasing a particular asset. Based on the law of supply and demand, which you can learn in chapter 4, the price rises when the demand for the product/asset is high.

The indicators of an impending bullish trend are, at times, unclear. That's why traders utilize technical analysis to recognize signals for a price increase. By researching and studying charts and indicators, you can predict price direction with a certain degree of accuracy. Technical indicators like MAs, RSI, and stochastic are also covered in the said chapter.

-What's a Bear Market?

When the market has experienced a prolonged price decrease, the condition is considered as a bear market. In contrast to bullish trends, a bear market arises when the value of an asset decline by 20%.

Like a bull market, a bear market is a condition. It applies to securities markets and individual assets. Recessions and other economic downturns are often accompanied by bear markets. You can also use the term to refer to any stock index or stock that has experienced a 20% decrease in value for the past 2 months.

Take the Nasdaq Composite bubble in 1999 as an example. Due to the bursting of the dot-com bubble, the value of the public shares being offered by Boo, Webvan, Pets.com, Worldcom, Global Crossing, Northpoint Communications dropped by over 30%. They fell into a bear market territory.

Many of the aforementioned entities closed their shutters forever.

Keep in mind that stock market correction and bear market are two different things, even though they're used interchangeably. A stock market correction occurs when a stock's value falls by 10%. A correction is upgraded to a bear market once the price decreases by 20% more.

Here are some factors that can cause corrections and bear markets:

- Stock market crash
- Recession
- Major economic events
- Investor fear and uncertainty
- A nation's poor credit rating
- Widespread investor speculation and irresponsible lending
- Over-leveraged investing
- Oil price movements

-Invest in a bear market

What's one of the secrets of day-traders? They don't only trade daily, but they also invest for the long-term. Adept day traders also engage in swing trading, especially for volatile assets that have the potential to increase in value in the coming months.

How do they do that? Here are some of their trading secrets and winning characteristics:

1. Thinking outside the box

When the value of a stock seems to decrease infinitely, traders, especially the beginners, tend to take sell positions before things get worse. As soon as they can, they try to get out of the market.

When a bull market arises and the price continues to rise, they often take a buy position. They fear of losing the chance to make a profit.

In electronic trading, many experts, including seasoned traders, like Geroge Soros and Paul Teodore Jones, sell high and buy low.

In chapter 5, it is explained why beginner traders should take advantage of sudden price changes and why they should choose the opposite of what the majority does.

2. Focusing on impactful indicators

Often, a big and influential company may go out of business when a bear market arises. That, in itself, is an indicator. When an economy goes bad, companies, as well as their share prices, are negatively affected.

On the other hand, trending and thriving companies over-perform and outperform their rivals. As a rule of thumb, focus on public shares of companies that are rock solid, well-rooted, and transparent.

The Tools You Need for Trading

Day trading, like swing and position trading, requires tools and services for mitigating risks and improving profitability. Foremost, you need a smartphone, personal computer, and internet connection.

Depending on your broker, you may also need a telephone and landline. This can come in handy if you have to urgently call your broker. For example, you can contact them if you encounter transaction errors or you need help from a CS representative.

A trading-charting platform showing real-time market data is needed for making highly accurate predictions and for timing your trades. Aside from these, day traders need various tools to support their active trading lifestyles. These can include desk items, software, and hardware:

> ➢ Day trading charting programs, like Ninja Trader

> ➢ Laptop or computer

> ➢ Telephone and landline

> ➢ Stable internet connection

> ➢ Backup internet access

> ➢ Timely market statistics

> ➢ App or web-based broker or brokerage platform

The items listed above are the most basic tools every day-trader needs. A fast and reliable personal computer or smartphone is a must. A trading charting program is also a necessity. A smartphone with a mobile plan or data can serve as a backup internet source and as a device for mobile charting and trading.

Aside from Ninja Trader, StockCharts and Trading View are also highly-rated charting software, according to Investopedia. Lastly, you need a prominent and trusted broker or brokerage firm. Without either of the two, you can't trade anything electronically.

Chapter Summary

Day trading can be a lucrative business. It can broaden your financial portfolio, keeping you away from bankruptcy. You can also combine it with other types of trading, like swing and position trading. Swing trading is a type of investing. Traders engage in it and take long positions for months at a time.

Day traders often opt for short positions, which are also referred to as sell positions. Most day traders exit the market every closing of a trading day. There are many electronic markets out there, namely the stocks exchanges, Forex markets, and options markets. Often, large financial entities can manipulate these markets.

By watching out for reversals, trends, and economic conditions, traders can make accurate predictions and execute profitable trades. In the next chapter, you'll learn how to observe trading markets, as well as the elements that drive them.

Step 2: Observing Market Behavior 101

Inflation, recession, and other adverse economic conditions generate negative news for the industry. This can adversely affect exchange rates and stock prices. However, if you know how to turn the tides in your favor, you can make a profit out of any economic event, whether good or bad.

Governing bodies, such as the US Federal Reserve Board (Fed) and the National Payments System, supervises the US government's executive branches. They're responsible for tax changes and fiscal policy moves. Simply put, they can minimize the detrimental effects of certain business cycles (e.g. expansion and recession) and promote economic growth to raise the value of the domestic currency and local stocks.

However, even such an authoritarian organization can't erase economic cycles. Traders and marketers anticipate business cycles with the intention to make profits.

In this chapter, you'll know which indicators affect trading cycles and how to understand economic and market conditions, as well as be able to read market sentiment. The insights you'll gain can help you understand the different strategies and analysis methods employed in day trading.

The Fundamentals of Business Cycles

Foremost, what's a business cycle? The business cycle is the natural fluctuations in economic growth. It occurs over time and is valuable for analyzing trends and making predictions.

The business cycle also refers to the upward and downward fluctuations of GDP or gross domestic product over a given time. Its alternate names are "trade cycle" and "economic cycle." Its duration is the period involving a single contraction and boom, in sequence.

The length of a cycle entails the amount of time it takes to complete a sequence. The sequence starts with a boom and ends with a compression. Each cycle has four phases:

1. Expansion

The expansion period takes place between the peak and the through. This is when the economy is growing nonstop. The GDP, the monetary measure that determines the economic output of a nation or economy, is steadily increasing. The growth rate of the gross domestic product ranges between 2% and 3%.

The unemployment rate is at its natural rate of 3.5% to 4.5%, while inflation is lesser than 2%. And, the value of most stocks is bullish--in a bull market. For a properly managed economy, it will be in this phase for years.

Expansion transitions to peak when the growth rate is over 3% and when the economy is overheating. In this period, inflation becomes greater than 2%. The inflation rate may also surpass 10%.

In such cases, multiple stock corrections become apparent. Investors and traders become irrationally exuberated, generating asset bubbles. What's this? An asset bubble is created when assets, like gold, stocks, and housing, experience a dramatic rise in value over a very short period.

The value of the asset doesn't support the bubble. Irrational exuberance--an economic phenomenon wherein many people are purchasing a specific type of asset--is a hallmark of an asset bubble. After the bubble forms, many even take loans just to invest in the asset. When thousands of investors flock to an asset, like real estate, its price and demand increase.

2. Peak

This is the second phase. Peak is the month(s) when expansion transitions into the recession or contraction phase. In this phase, the economy, along with the GDP, inflates at full speed.

The GDP, to be more specific, may reach its maximum output. Also, employment levels are also at all-time highs. Investors and businessmen are prospering.

However, inflation nears as salaries and prices increase. In such conditions, inflation may have already set in. High inflation can cause a recession.

3. Recession/Contraction

During a recession, the economy falls from peak. Employment rate decreases, and unemployment rate increases.

Eventually, output and production decline. Prices and wages stop increasing as well. It may not fall, but if the recession lasts for many years, then employment levels will continue to decline and salary rates start to fall.

4. Trough

This is the 4th phase and the month(s) when the country transitions from recession to the recovery phase, which is also considered as the expansion period. The trough is when the economy hits all-time bottom.

If this phase prolongs, it may lead to a depression. Depression, in economics, is a prolonged and severe recession. The trough marks the end of a business cycle.

When the economy grows again from rock bottom, output and employment start pick up. This period of recovery and expansion pulls and propels the country in question off the lowest level.

The period pushes the economy towards the next peak, and employment rate increases again. This makes the country's financial situation and credit rating look promising. Improving the economy, investors flock again to the nation to invest.

The Economic Indicators and Their Significance

Any economy goes through the four broad cycles mentioned above. In peak and expansion, the employment rate is high and many are optimistic. Financial prosperity is prevalent.

In the recession and trough phases, things become tougher, economically. Many lose their jobs and numerous businesses close their shutters forever. The end of a business cycle paves the way for a new one.

Economic indicators can help you determine where in the cycle an economy is and in what direction it's moving. Is a contraction near? Does the high employment rate in a country spells an inevitable recession?

With the help of economic indicators, you can find the answer to the questions above and other related inquiries. Most traders, specifically speculators and analysts, those who pore over both economic and financial information to evaluate outcomes and identify opportunities for investment and trading recommendations, tend to observe trends over several releases.

An economic calendar, which is a schedule of dates of significant events that can affect price action of securities and the status of markets, presents economic indicator data. Some brokers and trading platforms provide regularly updated economic calendars.

Here are the most important economic indicators that you should consider when you're observing market behavior:

> Commodity Price index

> National Employment

> Business Inventories

- Beige Book

- Core Pce Price Index

- Consumer Price Index

- CCI or Conference Board Consumer Confidence Index

- The number of orders for durable goods

- The number of home sales

- Employment Situation Report

- Employment Cost Index

- The number of factory orders

- GDP or Gross Domestic Product

- Housing Starts

- Ivey Purchasing Managers Index

- The results of Ism non-manufacturing and manufacturing surveys

- Initial Jobless Claims

- ➤ Industrial Capacity and Production Utilization

- ➤ Leaking Indicators

- ➤ NFP or Non-Farms Payrolls

- ➤ PMI or Purchasing Managers Index

- ➤ PPI or Producer Price Index

- ➤ Personal Income and Company Spending

- ➤ The total number of retail sales of the company in question

- ➤ Trade Balance, the net sum of a country's imports and exports of goods

- ➤ TIC or Treasury International Capital

- ➤ Tankan Survey

- ➤ MCSI or University of Michigan Consumer Sentiment

- ➤ Unemployment Rate

- ➤ The results of the ZEW Financial Market Survey

Please take note that some of the aforementioned indicators are only applicable to businesses/entities in their respective industries.

Indicators reveal important news and data that can affect markets, as well as tradable assets. Depending on the medium and virality of the news, it can impact the performance of stocks, currency prices, and trading volume.

As a day trader, you must watch and read economic news relevant to your target security and monitor financial market activities. With help from the right indicators, you can make accurate and profitable predictions. You can utilize an indicator for many sessions, but keep in mind that there are numerous ways of interpretation.

-Interest Rates

Watching the FEDs, as well as the entities, organizations, and authoritative people linked to them must be a daily habit for you. The FOMC or the Federal Open Market Committee includes the following:

> ➤ Seven members of the Board of Governors

> ➤ The president of 4 of 11 Federal Reserve Banks (State some names)

> ➤ The president of the New York Federal
> Reserve Bank

The FOMC is responsible for monitoring "open market operations." This is the primary tool whereby the FEDs execute US monetary policies. This, in turn, affects federal funds rate, credit conditions, and aggregate demand. In fact, it can affect the whole economy.

You must track what they may or may not do. This is in particular to interest rates since they can manipulate the country's current and future interest rates. The members meet eight times per year, but local newspapers, like the NY Times, and news websites, such as Forbes and Yahoo Finance, publish related stories on a daily or weekly basis.

Every time Ben Bernanke, the chairman of the FEDs, speaks publicly, journalists and various writers listen for indications and plans of the organizations. They also do the same for the other members. Journalists and news writers scrutinize and dissect every information the FEDs share with the public.

Press coverage summarizes the data shared and tell whether the Fed may lower or raise interest rates. Interest rates can significantly impact economies and how trades are made. A rate increase can decrease the spending of a nation.

This can lead to an economic slowdown. The FEDs raises interest rates if the economy is overheating.

In such conditions, inflation is imminent. Whether the board fears a downturn to the GDP or they're spurring growth during contraction, they will reduce interest rates to entice foreign investors and promote growth and spending.

Aside from economic news from reliable news outlets, you can also refer to the Beige Book. The US twelve Federal Reserve Banks compiles the data in the Beige Book. This includes the present economic conditions of the twelve districts.

Two weeks before each meeting, wherein monetary policies, which include interest rates, are set. The summaries in the Beige Book are developed through interviews with economists, market experts, business leaders, and other personalities familiar with the economy of the districts.

-Money Supply

An increase in a nation's money supply is a prime indicator of inflation. When this indicator is greater than the supply of goods, the inflation rate and prices go up. Money, stocks, and commodities traders must consider and vigilantly observe the following aggregates:

> Inflation

> Money Supply

> Goods & Services

In particular, the Federal Reserve Bank tracks two aggregates:

1. M1

M1 includes money utilized for payments, such as checking accounts in thrifts and banks and the circulating currency.

2. M2

M2 are the currencies sitting in bank deposits and bank vaults and those being kept in the money market and retail savings account. At www.federaalresesrve.gov/releases/h6/Current, you can follow the stock measures for M1 and M2.

-Deflation

Deflation is the opposite of inflation. When prices start falling, deflation can take center stage. It typically transpires when there's a prolonged period of a price decrease. The 1930 Great Depression is a classic example of deflation.

As mentioned in the section for "Money Supply," the prices of goods increase when the money supply is greater than goods being produced and circulated. In periods of deflation, improving the money supply won't likely be able to raise an economy in a downturn.

In such cases, adding more money to the economy can be risky. This is especially true when products are in excess and production continues although prices are falling. Japan's economic crisis in 2004 is a good example.

Even though Japan's central bank lowered its interest rates and printed more money to curb the price structure's downturn, the deflation continued until 2007. The 2011 Tohoku earthquake and tsunami have also negatively affected the nation's economy.

Deflation broadly impacted the Japanese economy in the Lost 30 Years, which is referred to as the period between 1991 and 2020. Between the mid-1990s and mid-2000s, Japan's Gross Domestic Product fell from $5.33 trillion to $4.36 trillion and regular wages fell by 5%.

In the last three decades, Japanese policymakers continued to try to curb the consequences. However, their efforts have little economic effect. In the 2000s, the country continued to print money, but the prices kept dropping in a deflationary spiral. Values of stocks, currency exchange rate, and housing and commodity prices continued to fall.

-Jobless Claims

The US Department of Labor reports Jobless claims statistics every week. This includes the number of people applying for unemployment insurance benefits. Jobless Claims are important indicators in knowing the health of an economy or the state of the employment situation of a country.

The report from the BLS or the US Bureau of Labor Statistics compiles the weekly Employment Situation Summary. This report is a critical economic indicator. It determines the expectations for the other statistics for that particular month. Take the scenario below as an example.

A weak labor market, which is usually reported in the summary, can be considered a strong sign of low retail sales and other negative reports. The Employment Situation Summary (ESS) also includes data broken down by industry, like manufacturing and construction.

A notable drop in the employment rate is an indication of a poor labor market. The report for housing starts will be negative. Housing starts is a key economic indicator. It lists new residential construction projects beginning during the given month.

The ESS and housing starts report can shock financial markets. This is particularly true when the numbers released are far from expectations. In this case, the value of some stocks, especially local public shares, could fall or rise.

The former can also happen when the employment rate is declining. Consequently, if the report indicates the opposite and reveals numbers better than the expected stats, the value of stocks will rise for a specific period. Remember, nothing is permanent in the markets.

Employment reports can strongly drive markets. Data and statistics reports hold recent assessments of many sectors and industries. The ESS is considered the best indicator for wage pressure and unemployment.

The rise of the unemployment rate is one of the initial signs of impending national inflation. Additionally, the report covers the labor markets of the United States' entire 250 regions and each major industry.

The Labor Department's website (www.bls.gov) releases a report on the first Friday of every month at 8:30 a.m. Four of the most important parts of the report are as follows:

> Unemployment rate

> Average earnings

> Average weekly hours

> The number of new jobs created

-Employment Cost Index

The ECI or the Employment Cost Index is also a type of BLS survey of employer payrolls. Every quarter, it measures and presents the changes in total employee compensation in every region. Various employers, investors, economists, and stockholders use the ECI indicator to track the health of the economy in question. The BLS surveys over 3,000 private firms and more than 500 local governments. The report is released every last business day of January, April, July, and October.

-Consumer Confidence

Consumer confidence is defined as the statistical measure of consumer sentiments about the future and current economic conditions. Like the ECI, it's utilized to measure an economy's health. With this indicator, you can take a glimpse at the future of a market.

When the performance is high, spending will increase. The CCI or the Consumer Confidence Index is the best index when monitoring this indicator. The US Conference Board publishes this report by surveying 5,000 households every three to six months.

When confidence is low, the Federal Reserve Banks will lower interest rates. This positively impacts stock markets. High confidence levels, on the other hand, are warning signs of a possible near contraction period. In the early phase of recession or before it, the Feds may raise interest rates in a last-ditch attempt to curb inflation rates. When interest rates are increased, the prices of stocks decrease.

The US Conference Board releases the CCI at 10 a.m. on the last Tuesday of each month. You can track the monthly results at their website www.conference-board.org. Go to the "Economics" section and hover towards the "Consumer Confidence" tab.

How to Use the Data You've Gathered

Indeed, various data is available for both fundamental analysis and technical analysis, which are discussed in the next chapters. However, not every piece of information you've collected is relevant to the type of security you want to trade. Organizing your collection of relevant data for reading charts and tracking trends will allow you to easily analyze phases of the business cycle and wisely choose economic signs.

Now, here are the steps you should take so that your every effort would be fruitful and bear relevant results:

1. Maintain your economic calendar

Above all else, you must maintain your economic calendar for the release dates of relevant indicators. Therefore, always watch trends and the rise and fall of security prices when a key indicator is soon to be released. In chapter 5, you can learn how to read trends and patterns.

2. Determine the industries and parts of the economy that will be impacted by the indicators

The GDP, for example, suggests the future path of economic growth. CPI and PPI, on the other hand, are strong measures of inflation. With these two, you'll have the ability to know the current phase of the business cycle and make accurate predictions about price movements.

3. Scrutinize the crucial parts of your chosen indicators

Like economies, indicators also have parts. Ask yourself, "what part of the index is critical to my future decisions?"

For instance, the CPI's energy and food components are often highly volatile. Hence, for stock trading, CPI's core bears the most important numbers.

4.   Check for revisions in new indicators

Often, indicators are revised. The changes may be not that significant, but that small modification may reveal a small shift in the cycle. So, always check for revisions and know how the changes impact monthly trends.

5.   Watch the trends

On your economic calendar, track the major parts of each indicator you're watching. Monitor the trends of the relevant data components so that you can accurately predict the state of the economy and the current phase of the business cycle. Examples include indices, earnings report, and economic summaries, like industrial production and consumer leverage ratio.

Chapter Summary

Economic indicators, when used properly, provide valuable data for analysis and interpreting future and current trading possibilities. Usually employed in fundamental analysis, economic indicators aid in judging the health of an economy and for determining the phase in a business cycle.

Various indicator data are available online and on economic reports, which are published periodically. You need to be adverse in choosing the right indicators to produce desirable results from your analyses and trades. In the next chapter, you can learn how to do that and conduct fundamental analysis.

Step 3: Getting Acquainted with Fundamental Analysis

It's time for fundamental analysis! FA or fundamental analysis measures an asset's intrinsic value, by examining and observing relevant financial and economic indicators. From macroeconomic factors, like industry conditions to Employment Situation Reports, fundamental analysis involves anything that affects, whether negatively or positively, the value of a security.

The end goal of FA is to come up with a highly accurate figure that a trader can compare with the asset's present price for overvaluation or undervaluation. This stock analysis method is quite the opposite of technical analysis, which is detailed in the next chapter: "Understanding Technical Analysis."

The Importance of Fundamental Analysis

The fundamentals include market and economic conditions that can impact a tradable asset. It also covers the financial data of company activities and information about their failures and successes.

With fundamental analysis, you'll have the ability to know differences in the stock prices of two or more companies using earnings growth, business conditions, and other factors. These are discussed in the succeeding sections.

FA can provide consistent and reliable information. Using this type of analysis, you can evaluate a financial security's intrinsic value. This is the trading price or the net worth of an asset.

For example, the discounted cash flow model is employed when determining a company's weighted average capital and free cash flow. The average capital accounts for the present value of money. The DCF model can determine the present value of a stock by forecasting the cash flow and discounting it. The model employs a discount rate to calculate the DCF.

If the DCF figure is over the present investment cost, then opportunities could give rise to positive returns. Typically, companies employ the capital's weighted average cost. This includes the stockholder's expected rate of return.

The market price (intrinsic value) can be compared to the asset's trading value. If the security being traded is less than its actual book value, you should purchase that asset. This type of trading is called Value Investing.

Benjamin Graham, the late American economist and successful investor, is the father of Value Investing. Warren Buffet, the largest shareholder of Berkshire Hathaway, popularized the said investment strategy, which involves excessive use of fundamental analysis.

That's just one of the significance of FA.

Where to Start

1. To begin, choose a business sector or industry that is relevant to your preferred stock.

2. Research the major players of the company offering the public share. Look at the fundamentals of the sector or industry. For example, the business components of the hospitality industry include safety, sales, finance, maintenance, event management, and office operations.

3. Reduce the list of the firms you want to compare with the company. You should also look at the daily trading volume of the security. If it has a low number of daily trades, then it will be hard for you to get out of a position.

The tools utilized in FA require the comparison of at least two companies within the industry in question.

Here are some of the tools you can use:

- EPS or Earnings per Share

- (P/E) ratio or price-to-earnings ratio

- Return on equity

- (P/B) or price-to-book ration

- Price-to-sales ratio

- Beta

- Projected earnings growth

- Dividend yield ratio

- Dividend payout ratio

For discussion purposes, consider two giant firms in the home improvement sector: Lowe's and Home Depot. After the 2007 stock market crash, both companies experienced a downturn in their public shares.

As a result, they halted expansion, waited for the next phase in the business cycle, and the value of their stocks fell in a spiraling downtrend. That time, before the price gets any worse, many investors and day traders get out of the market.

They sold their public shares. Through fundamental analysis, they had predicted that the prices will get worse. They had also taken note of the impending bubble burst. For them to gain such insight, they scrutinized the companies' balance sheets and cash flow statements.

By considering the following section, you will learn how to read critical financial statements that can help determine intrinsic values in an asset. Acquiring such a skill is essential in day trading stocks.

-The income statement

In general, the income statement is a snapshot of the earnings and their impacts on the company's bottom line-- the net income after all expenses, which include income taxes, interest charges, and administrative costs, are removed. The income statement is where a public firm states its costs and revenues.

With the income statement (P&L), you can ascertain the effects of taxes, depreciation, and interest of the entity in question and forecast its earnings potential. Every P&L has three important sections: income, revenue, and expenses. The last section (expenses) includes depreciation costs. This is the portion of an asset considered consumed in the present period.

-How to read a financial statement

1. Check all the figures if they're right.

2. Find or calculate the bottom line.

3. Scrutinize the entity's various sources of income.

4. Examine the amounts and determine the biggest expenses.

5. Compare month-over-month and year-over-year numbers

6. Think of the logical relationships between the numbers.

A year's worth of numbers will not reveal much. Hence, it's more effective to look at the trends throughout several years so that you can accurately predict growth potential and assess the current financial state of the company. Doing so also determines how well the entity is doing against its competitors.

Both annual and quarterly reports are important. Differentiating their results on a year-to-year or quarter-to-quarter basis enables you to specify the financial health of the company for every month. In doing so, you can know which dates are the most efficient for day trading.

For example, by examining the reports for Q1 of 2018 versus the results for Q1 2019, you know whether its earnings are decreasing or increasing. For most companies, Q1 is productive, but for others, like retail chains, Q4 brings in a lot of profits. Hence, you may need results for every quarter especially if the asset requires it.

Annual income statements, on the other hand, present a summary of the earnings or losses for a whole year. Public companies, like Lowe's and Tesla, are required to file yearly and quarterly financial reports with the Securities Exchange Commission (SEC).

-Revenues

Sales revenues present the company's overall sales within a specific period before expenses are subtracted. However, some firms, like Nike and Salesforce, only reports net sales on their income statements. From collected figures, you can see growth or decline in revenues.

-Cost of goods sold (COGS)

COGS or cost of services sold is a measure that shows the net costs directly related to the firm's services or products.

This includes freight charges, purchase discounts, and other expenses related to the act of selling.

-Expenses

The expenses portion includes the administrative costs, sales costs, and operating costs of the business. Expenses shouldn't be higher than the gross profits. Low expenses figures are good signs, and they could mean excellent growth potential.

-Interest payments

This portion of the income statement presents the short-term financial health of the company. It mainly includes tax-deductible costs. To determine the entity's fiscal health, use the EBIT number or the earnings before interest and taxes, as well as the interest expense number.

Here are some key points for this type of financial statement:

1. To calculate the interest coverage ratio, divide the interest expenses with the EBIT number. Those with high coverage ratios can easily meet their loan obligations.

2. By subtracting the tax and interest expenses from the operating income, you can determine the short-term

financial health of the company. You can use the result to know whether or not the entity generates enough income to pay its interest payments.

3. Comparing the ratios of different companies within the same sector is an effective way to judge or gauge the ratios' values.

4. Well-refuted analysts, including George Soros and Richard Dennis, consider number 3 as a poor interest coverage ratio. It generally means that the public company is buried in debt or will be in trouble shortly.

-Dividend Payments

Some companies pay dividends. This is a part of a percentage of the profits that the firm makes. The amount depends on the investor's share of common stock. The shareholders receive their dividends once every quarter in a year.

Hence, the shareholders receive dividends at least four times a year. The company needs to have a good cash flow to make dividend payments. Examining its historical and present dividend payouts allows you to gauge its financial strength for fundamental analysis.

-Testing Profitability

Profitability ratios are utilized to assess a business' capability to generate profit relative to its assets, revenues, operating costs, shareholders' equity, or balance sheet assets. Testing profitability can reveal how a firm efficiently generates value and profit for shareholders.

As financial metrics, they can determine whether or not the company can provide dividend payments.

For computation, the net profit margin and operating margin are used. The former looks at earnings less the expenses. The latter considers profits from operations before tax and interest expenses.

The formula for both metrics are listed below:

Net profit margin = earnings after taxes/net sales or gross profit

Operating margin = operating income/net sales or gross profit

A higher ratio implies that the company has an excellent industry average and historical performance. Like the previous aforementioned metrics, you can also use profitability ratios when comparing two or more companies.

-Cash Flow Statements

A cash flow statement (CFS) is a valuable measure of profitability, strength, and future outlook. It can determine whether or not the business can pay its expenses and loan interests.

Here are the formulas:

Free Cash Flow = Net income + Depreciation/Amortization - Change in Working Capital - Principal Expenditure

Cash Flow Forecast = Beginning Cash + Estimated Inflows - Estimated Outflows = End Cash

Cash Flow from Operations = Operating Income + Depreciation - Tax Payments + Change in Working Capital

-Depreciation

In accounting, depreciation is considered an expense. It relates to an entity's fixed assets. It represents the usage of assets each accounting period, which could either be a fiscal or calendar year. It could also be a week, a quarter, or a month. Various assets incur depreciation. A few examples include equipment, vehicles, and facilities.

When public companies pay for a valuable item or equipment, they record it as an asset, which represents long-term value for a company. Using the asset creates distorted net income. That's why each use is recorded or estimated.

A variety of depreciation formulas are available for accounting and analysis methods. The most relevant to fundamental analysis are listed below:

Unit of Product Method = Asset Cost - Salvage Value/Useful Life in the Form of Units Produced

Depreciation Per Year = Asset Cost - Salvage Value/Asset's Useful Life

Straight Line Depreciation Method = Asset Cost - Residual Value/Asset's Useful Life

Companies, especially those offering public shares, report asset depreciation to stakeholders. It also allows them to cover the asset's net cost over its entire lifespan, rather than immediately recovering the cost of purchase. This enables firms to replace assets with the right amount of revenue.

-Investment activity

This part of the income statement represents how the public company spends its funds for growing and establishing long-term assets, like new buildings and property acquisitions. The investment activity section also covers the sales of large assets and equity investments. By tracking such activities, you can forecast the result of the entity's long-term planning and capital planning activities.

Learning How to Read the Balance Sheet

The balance sheet presents the company's liabilities and assets at a specific period. Unlike the financial statement, which shows a company's operating results, a balance sheet covers the property and liabilities of a public company.

The value that the company takes in is balanced out against its liabilities. Please keep in mind that when liabilities equal assets plus equity, the financial statement is considered *balanced.*

Each balance sheet has three sections:

1. Assets

This part details everything that the firm owns

2. Liabilities

The liabilities section includes the debts and other debtor claims on the company.

3. Shareholder's equity

Also referred to as owner's equity, this section lists all claims made by investors and owners.

The balance sheet details assets and liabilities according to liquidity, or how easily and quickly you can convert them to cash. The most liquid liabilities and assets are sorted first on the list. The long-term items appear last.

The asset section is divided into two parts:

1. Current assets

Current assets are the valuable resources that are exhausted in one year, like accounts receivable, supplies, and inventory.

2. Long-term assets

These have lifespans of more than one year. Fixtures, equipment, and buildings are examples of long-term assets.

The liabilities portion is also divided into two parts:

1. Short-term liabilities

Short-term liabilities include customer deposits, dividends payable, taxes payable, accrued expenses, and trade accounts payable.

2. Long-term liabilities

Non-current liabilities are due beyond a year. Some examples are deferred revenues, deferred compensation, deferred income taxes, and post-retirement healthcare liabilities.

How to Analyze Assets

When analyzing assets, you've to consider two prime ratios so that you can tell how the company collects accounts receivable (accounts receivable turnover) and how they deplete their inventory (inventory turnover).

For the latter, a two-step process is involved:

1. To know how quickly the entity converts its accounts receivable turnover into cash, use the formula below:

Accounts Receivable Turnover = Sales on Account/Average Accounts

2. Next, you need to determine how quickly the entity collects on its accounts. To do this, divide the quotient of

the above formula by 365. Doing this allows you to find the total number of days they take to collect on accounts.

Inventory turnover testing involves a similar process:

1. For a specific year, you can find out the ratio by using the formula below:

Inventory Turnover Ratio = CGS or Cost of Goods Sold/Average Inventory

2. Then, divide the quotient by 365. The result tells the average number of days that the firm turns over its inventory.

The quicker the entity finishes its operations or sells its inventory, the better it's handling its assets. By following the aforementioned steps and using the formulas, you can compare the key entities within the industry. This allows you to tell whether the target company is competitive or not.

In contrast, an increasing accounts receivable turnover ratio is considered a red flag. It signals that the entity is facing cash problems. When inventory numbers are increasing or stagnant, that public company isn't selling its products well.

-Considering Debt

Debt is everything that a company owes. It's a type of deferred payment. When planning to make a trade, there are two ratios that you must look at that are directly linked to the company's debt:

-Current Ratio

The current ratio measures the ability of the entity to pay its short-term debts. It tells analysts how the firm can maximize current assets on its balance sheet for satisfying payables, like current debt. The higher the ratio is, the more short-term liquidity the entity has. A value less than 1 may indicate poor liquidity, which suggests an inability to pay short-term liabilities.

By scrutinizing the balance sheet, you can use the formula below to get the current ratio:

Current Ratio = Present Assets/Present Liabilities

-Quick or Acid Ratio

This measure indicates the capacity of the company to pay its present liabilities without having to sell items from its inventory. It also doesn't involve additional financing. The formula to get the acid ratio is listed below:

Quick Ratio = Present Assets - Current Inventory/Current Liabilities

Once you have calculated the two measures above, compare the results of your target company to that of its competitors. On your list, only include entities that are in the same industry.

When the current ratio is lower than that of other key rivals, then that public company is facing difficulty paying off short-term debts. This is a very strong signal that bankruptcy is near. A higher current ratio is a bad sign as well since it might indicate poor asset utilization.

Hence, day traders positively view companies that have ratios close to the industry average. Some companies release their ratios to the public. Lowe's and Home Depot do this.

For example, 1:1 is a good acid test ratio since it indicates a good credit risk. Any entity that is having difficulty paying short-term liabilities may not meet all of its short-term obligations in the future. When this is fairly obvious, the share price of the company will drop.

How to Employ Fundamental Analysis

You now know all the indicators that will prove beneficial to your trading endeavors. So, it's time to learn how to actually use fundamental analysis using your preferred economic indicators.

1. The very first step to take is to create a list of profitable stocks you can research. You can use a Stock Screener to filter stocks based on dividend ratio, P/E ratio, sector, or earnings per share. Some of the best free web-based stock screeners are listed below:

- ➢ Yahoo! Finance

- ➢ Chart Mill

- ➢ Zacks

- ➢ StoclFetcher

- ➢ Google Finance

- ➢ Stock Rover

> FinViz

To limit the results, use the Search option by one criterion at a time.

2. Once you've made a list, research more by examining financial statements. Analyze growth rate, balance sheets, net income, and profit and losses. Several years of growth is a good indicator, while too much debt is a red flag.

3. After that, research their services or products. Do they have something unique? Within the industry, are they competitive enough? If you're aiming to day trade or swing trade using a public share, then consider the future prospects of your target company.

4. Although this step is optional, it can prove to be beneficial especially when there are newly elected executives, managers, or board members. Find the answers to the following questions:

> What's their work history?

> Do they have a reputation for failure or success with other firms?

When trading stocks, which makes the best use of fundamental analysis, you're putting your hard-earned savings in the hands of executives. So, it's best to consider this step.

When everything is taken into account, you'll probably end up with just a handful of potential candidates for your Mula! From here, you can start devising your trading plan and employing your trading system. These are further discussed in chapter 4.

On Stock Valuations

In this section, let's talk about how to use everything you've calculated and collected. This can help you decide the right price of a share.

Typically, the stock's value is the amount that traders are willing to pay for it. If no one is willing to buy an overpriced stock, many positions taken for that stock will stay open until someone makes a purchase or the owner of the stock voluntarily closes it.

For highly liquid assets, their actual value fluctuates throughout the day. This is especially true when its trading volume is quite high. FA is a tool that day traders utilize to analyze the following:

> Future business plans

> Market share

> Revenue growth

> Annual and monthly earnings

Fundamental analysis allows traders and investors to determine the right price for a stock. If it's currently overpriced in the market, then only beginners will be enticed to take the deal.

Likewise, the fair value can be determined with fundamental analysis. Therefore, you can ascertain if an offer is below the average price (fair value). This is a good deal. If you think the trade price won't go any lower, then it's best to grab such a bargain. Basically, FA analyzes financial security to specify its fair value (intrinsic value) by the evaluation of non-financial, financial, and economic factors.

The Six Fundamental Analysis Tools

Aside from the measures and ratios mentioned above, here are more tools that can greatly aid in fundamental analysis. Many trading platforms offer free tools such as EPS and P/E Ratio. You can employ the tools below to maximize the benefits of your economic calendar. With them, you won't be trading blind.

-Earnings Per Share

EPS or earnings per share refers to the profits allotted to each outstanding share. You can use two formulas to compute EPS:

Earnings per Share = Net Income/Total Number of Outstanding Shares

Earnings per Share = Net Income/Weighted Average of Outstanding Shares

-P/E Ratio

P/E ratio stands for price-to-earnings ratio. This tool. enables you to look at the link between EPS and the price of a particular stock. Based on earnings, it presents the entity's value, as well as market expectations. To calculate the P/E ratio, use the formula below:

Price to Earnings Ratio = Market Value or Stock Price/EPS

-PEG Ratio

By using PEG or price-to-growth ratio, you can determine the value of the stock in question while being able to consider earnings growth. The formula of this measure is listed below:

PEG Ratio = P/E Ratio/Earnings Growth Rate

Once you have the P/E Ratio, you can easily compute this measure. Just divide the price-to-earnings ratio by the growth rate of the company's net earnings within a given period.

-P/B Ratio

The P/B Ratio determines the present book value per share relative to the market value of the stock. The book value is the company's total assets less the present liabilities. It serves as an excellent indicator of undervalued stocks.

Here's the formula for the price-to-book ratio:

P/B Ratio = Market Value per Share/Book Value per Share

-Dividend Payout Ratio

This is also referred to as the payout ratio. It can help you know dividends that are issued to shareholders relative to the entity's net income. By calculating the dividend payout ratio, you can figure out how much shareholders receive from their investment.

To be exact, the dividend payout ratio determines how much dividend is paid on a quarterly or annual basis. Unlike other fundamental tools, a low payout rate isn't a red flag. This is especially true if the company is investing retained funds for future growth.

For the formula, please refer to the following equation:

Dividend Payout Ratio = Net Income/Dividends Paid

-Dividends Yield

This the ratio of the yearly dividend relative to the price per share. A high dividend yield ratio may indicate growth and high earnings. To calculate dividend yield, please refer to the formula below:

Dividend Yield = Yearly Dividend/Present Share Price

-Return on Equity

ROE stands for return on equity. It measures an entity's performance base on its shareholder's equity and net income. Using it on fundamental analysis allows you to reveal whether or not a company is using its assets effectively in generating profits. The formula goes like this:

ROE = Net Income/Average Shareholder Equity

When to Use Fundamental Analysis?

With due diligence and intensive research, you can make smart trades, in which you minimize your losses and maximizes your winnings. Domestic currencies don't have fundamentals. That's why most use technical analysis in Forex trading. In the next chapter "Understanding Technical Analysis," there are many in-depth lessons for the topic. However, if you prefer to trade dividends and company shares, then choose fundamental analysis.

Step 4: Understanding Technical Analysis

Here's a technical analysis! Are you confused about the difference between TA and FA? This chapter is here to clear that up, but it offers more than that. If fundamental analysis deals with intrinsic values, technical analysis is for trends and price action--the changes in the value of a security over time.

Those are the focus of technical analysis. As time passes, prices fall and trends become apparent. Patterns can last until they reverse or change due to news or catalyst. In trading, history can also repeat itself. Technical analysis focuses on price action and historical data.

When you finish this chapter, you can be a technician because you will acquire the skills necessary for conducting technical analysis, reading trends in price movements, and making accurate predictions. Technician is another term for technical analyst. You can start with using market statistics and price charts to devise an effective trading plan.

Getting Started

Technical analysis is utilized to identify events that will likely occur. To identify trends, technicians use logical frameworks.

They also use logical frameworks to look for breakouts and trading ranges. You'll learn more about these terms in the next sections.

To understand the methods of technicians, you need to be acquainted with the following technical analysis concepts:

> Imbalances between demand and supply cause fluctuations in prices.

> Price actions aren't always random.

> Everything is in the price.

You can Find Everything in the Price

Unlike FA, technical analysis isn't concerned with fundamental indicators, such as the latest financial statements or analyst's report. Hence, the factors integral to FA aren't involved in technical analysis.

Financial analysts scrutinize the present, future, and past prices of securities. They greatly emphasize and scrutinize historical price data.

Technicians, on the other hand, focus on what the price represents. They base their predictions and trades on what they see.

Nevertheless, you can combine TA and FA for optimum strategy. You will learn how to do this in the later sections of this chapter.

Price Actions Aren't Always Random

At times, prices increase, and often, if the indicators are in favor of them, they keep increasing until they reach the ceiling price for the day.

Of course, they can also decrease, and their values fluctuate. When they move in a specific direction over time, you can say that there's a "trend."

Random price actions can appear between trending moments. If you magnify price movements, you can see that trading ranges are formed by several mini trends. The more you zoom in, the more you can see that prices aren't always random.

Looking at Intraday

Basically, TA identifies periods during the occurrence of trends. Generally, technical traders base their trades on trending markets. They try to determine when trends will start or when they'll end. They either focus on mini-trends or long-lasting trends. Others do both.

When observing intraday (i.e., occurring within the day) price charts, you can view examples of trading ranges and mini trends. However, the two aforementioned elements on price-charts are useless for investors and swing traders. They're those who tend to take long positions for months at a time.

To be honest, it's impossible to exactly know, with 100% accuracy, which way a price of a security will move. Nevertheless, you can make an educated guess with almost a hundred percent certainty. With technical analysis, you can get to that money-making prediction.

Remember, history repeats itself. When stocks make familiar patterns, the same trend, which was notable in the past, could occur again.

In trading, the study of the past can help understand how prices and markets move. Patterns in price fluctuations repeat again and again. As a trader, your main task is to prepare for the next obvious opportunity to make money.

The 3 Most Important Components

Charts, patterns, and indicators are vital to TA. Patterns can't exist without a chart. You can't spot one without a chart. This shows and helps you visualize price movements and the patterns they form. Having a charting platform or application can make trading easier.

Please keep that in mind when you're choosing a broker. In case your preferred platform doesn't have a charting system, then use a real-time securities scanner.

For example, Investagram and StocksToTrade, two real-time stock scanners, can be used for charting and technical analysis. These apps also offer a Paper Trading feature. This allows for trading and pattern spotting simulations. Such features can be valuable to beginner traders.

Technical Analysis: The Complete Step-by-Step Guide

1. Understanding the theories behind TA

Based on Charles Dow's theories about the stock market, technical analysis was conceptualized. For decades, it has guided the approach of technicians towards financial markets. The theories are described below with details of how they're interpreted for technical analysis.

-Market changes reflect all known data

Technicians infer that the price movements of a financial security and its trading volume represent all available information needed to make highly accurate predictions. Hence, price listings can be considered as fair value, a broad measure of an asset's worth.

-Price actions can often be predicted and charted

As mentioned earlier, prices can move randomly. However, there are times when their movements are predictable. With every identified trend, an opportunity to make money arises.

There are many trading strategies out there. You may buy low and sell high during a bull market or sell short during a bear market when prices are falling. If you further adjust the duration for analysis, you may spot long- and short-term trends.

-History will repeat itself

According to Investopedia, the majority of traders and investors don't change their trading habits, strategies, and motivations overnight. You can expect that they'll exhibit repetitive behaviors to familiar conditions. Their behaviors can affect the market they're in since they and their motivations can collectively affect future price actions.

You can use this knowledge to profit from every historical trend that repeats itself. It's evident that TA regards market behavior and human actions even though it avoids intrinsic values.

The aforementioned trading principles are not at all times appropriate; however, many traders, including Tim Sykes, Warren Buffet, and Ross Cameron, consider them as their maxims. Look at them now. They're one of the richest people in the world. Buffet, in particular, is in Forbes' top 100 wealthiest men.

2. Look for Instant Results

Unlike FA, which considers financial data and balance sheets, TA focuses on periods as short as few minutes and no longer than four weeks. According to Bloomberg Businessweek, technical analysis is suitable for people who take short positions such as day traders.

3. Spot trends by reading charts

Technicians generally look at graphs and charts of security prices. They try to spot the future direction of the value of their target asset while overlooking individual fluctuations. Technical analysts classify trends by duration and type:

-Uptrends

Uptrends are characterized by lows and highs that become progressively higher. Like other types of trends, uptrends are also composed of mini trends.

-Downtrends

These are the opposite of uptrends. You can spot mini trends if you use a magnification tool. Successive lows and highs that are progressive lower characterize downtrends.

-Horizontal trends

Horizontal trends have a consistent direction, which is in an almost straight line. These faults change from previous price fluctuations. When the forces of demand and supply are almost equal, horizontal or sideway trends occur. This is common during periods of consolidation.

-Trend lines

Trend lines connect successive maximum highs, point by point. Drawing trend lines streamlines the process of spotting trends. Trend lines are also referred to as "channel lines."

-Intermediates trends

Intermediate trends last for at least 30 days, but they don't last for more than a year. They are consist of near-term trends.

-Near-term trends

Near-term trends last for at least a month. Major trends are comprised of intermediate and near-term trends.

-Major trends

These last longer for more than 12 months. Often, major trends don't have a consistent direction. For example, a two-week-long bull market could suddenly plummet and become a bear market in the 3rd week. This could last for more than 3 weeks. The bull market is a near-term trend, while the bear market is an example of an intermediate trend.

-The four charts

Technicians utilize four types of charts:

a) Line charts are for closing positions over a period.

b) Bar and candlestick charts are used for visualizing low and high prices between periods and for whole trading periods.

c) Point and figure charts show noteworthy price actions over a given time frame.

Over the years, since the conceptualization of technical analysis, technicians and traders have coined the aforementioned phrases for patterns appearing on charts used for TA.

Here are some more noteworthy trends to consider:

➢ A pattern or trend that resembles a cup with a handle often indicates that an upward trend may continue after a short correction.

➢ A saucer or downward bottom trend indicates a long period of bottoming before a significant uptrend.

➢ A double bottom or double top pattern indicates two failed attempts to surpass a low or high price. A reversal trend often follows this.

> ➢ In the same way, a triple bottom or triple top shows three failed attempts. They also precede a reversal.

4. Know support and resistance

Support and resistance are widely used concepts in currency trading. Check out the diagram below. The upward zigzag pattern looks like a bull market. When price reaches a peak and immediately pulls back, the point at the peak is known as the "resistance." The lowest point is called "support." A trend is made up of many supports and resistances. Resistances suggest that there will be a seller surplus. Support levels, on the other hand, indicate an impending buyer surplus. In this regard resistance and support are continuously formed whether the price generally moves up or down. Hence, this remains true during an uptrend or downtrend.

Traders trade the "bounce." "To buy a bounce" means you're purchasing a financial security after its value has reached a support level. This can bring forth a secondary movement that allows traders to make a profit from the

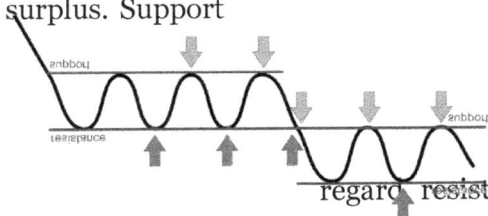

short-term correction. Aside from bounce trading, the following strategies also make use of support and resistance levels:

a) Take a buy position when the price falls or is falling towards the support

b) Take a sell position when the price rises or is rising towards the resistance

c) Sell when the price of the asset breaks up through the support level

d) Make a purchase when the price of the security breaks up through resistance

-How to Plot Support and Resistance

Support and resistance levels aren't exact numbers. Often, you'll see one of them with a figure that appears broken. On candlestick charts, like the example below, tests are represented by shadows that appear like candlesticks.

The shadows tested the support level, which is not a whole number. In such cases, the market is "breaking support," and the market is just testing that level or is being tested.

In TA, a test is when an asset's price nears an established resistance or support. If the price stays within the support and resistance levels, you can say that the test passes. If the price reaches new highs or new lows, then it fails.

What's the purpose of this? The results of such tests determine the accuracy of signals and patterns. These are the distinctive formations in price movements on a chart. Patterns serve as the foundation of technical analysis. They connect common price points, like highs and lows or closing prices, in a given period. In general, traders and analysts utilize tests to confirm support and resistance levels in a stock, currency, or other security.

-Indication of Broken Support and Resistance Levels

There is no definite answer to this. Some traders claim levels are considered broken when the asset's value can close past that level. When plotting levels of supports and resistances, avoid breakouts and decimals. Instead, focus on intentional movements and whole numbers as much as you can.

Please check out the chart below. In the example, it's best to plot the points around areas that form valleys or peaks. These are the lows and the highs respectively.

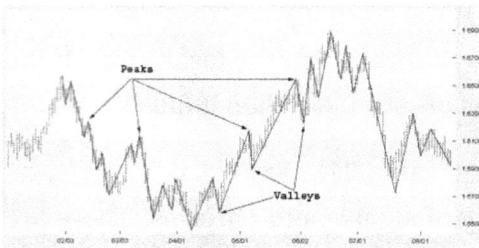

-Snippets About Support and Resistance

a) When the asset's price passes through a resistance level or the highest point on the chart, that resistance may become support soon.

b) A breakout is a price moving outside a predefined resistance or support level, with increased volume. Breakout traders take a long position after the price surpasses the resistance level. They take a short position when the price breaks below support.

c) MACD and RSI indicators, which are discussed in the following sections, are used to measure the strength of a breakout.

d) When a level is surpassed, the strength of follow-through depends on how strong the resistance or support break out is.

e) The support is the lowest value a financial security attains before many buyers take advantage of the situation, come in, and make purchases. This moves the price upwards.

f) Resistance is the highest value a financial instrument reaches before traders start selling and cause another price decrease. This is more commonly known as the "ceiling price."

In conclusion, the floor price is the bottom line of the given asset. It's also called the support level, and the ceiling price is the resistance level. These terms are used for the confirmation of a pattern or trend and for determining when is the next reversal.

5. Study the Trading Volume

Once you're done looking at trends, you must consider the trading volume of the asset in question. Doing so further validates the existence of the trend and helps in predicting when is the exact reversal. If the volume rises or falls slightly as the asset's value goes up, then the trend is valid and may soon experience a reversal.

-How to measure trading volume with technical analysis?

Trading volume measures how much specific security has been traded in a given period. For example, the volume of stocks is measured in the number of public shares traded.

For options and futures, the trading volume is based on how many contracts or CFDs have changed hands. Indicators and figures using volume data are provided with online charts.

Observing patterns in trading volume can give you an insight into the conviction and strength behind the trends in specific securities and entire markets. The same can be said for options and futures day trading. The volume in the said markets serves as an *indicator* of the market sentiment of the participants.

Volume plays an integral role in TA since it also features prominent technical indicators:

> ➢ Volume can help you measure the number of public shares/futures/options being traded in a stock or contracts.

> ➢ Speculators consider volume as an indicator of market strength. Rising markets with increasing volume are viewed as healthy and strong.

> ➢ When prices are falling while volume is increasing, the trend on the chart is getting ready for bottoming.

> ➢ When prices reach highs while volume is decreasing, a reversal may be taking shape. Watch out for this.

> ➢ The Klinger indicator and the on-balance volume are some charting tools based on trading volume.

6. Filter Minor Fluctuations by Using MAs

MAs stand for moving averages. An MA is a series of measured averages. They're calculated over equal periods.

The goal of this step is to remove irrelevant lows and highs and to streamline the whole technical analysis process. To be specific, it can help in reading overall patterns/trends.

Plotting prices against MAs makes it easy to spot reversals. You can use many methods for calculating averages to do this:

-Finding the SMA

SMA or simple moving average can be calculated by adding every closing price of a specific period. Then, divide the sum by the total number of addends.

-Finding the LMA

LMA stands for linear weighted average. To calculate LMA, list each price in a given period and multiply them by their position. After that, add all of the plotted prices together. Next, you must divide the sum by the number of addends. For example, over 4 days, the 1st price is multiplied by one, the 2nd is multiplied by two, and so forth.

-Finding the EMA

EMA or exponential moving average can be compared to the LMA. It weighs the latest prices. To calculate EMA, please follow the instructions below:

1) Calculate the simple moving average

2) Compute the multiplier for weighting the EMA

3) Lastly, calculate the present EMA

The calculation for the SMA is similar to computing a mean or average. That is to say, the simple moving average for any time periods is the sum of the closing prices for the time period. The sum is then divided by that same number.

For example, a 5-day SMA is the sum of the closing prices for the last 5 days, divided by 5.

7. Use Oscillators and Indicators to Support Your Findings

In technical analysis, indicators are considered calculations. They support the data collected from trends on a line chart, which are gleaned from the movements of prices. The use of indicators can increase the accuracy of your predictions. The MAs described in the previous step are an indicator. It's possible for indicators to have decimals. Others are limited to a range, like 1 to 100.

To better understand oscillators and indicators, please check out the key points below.

-Indicators may either be lagging or leading. Leading indicators can predict price actions and are useful when reading horizontal trends. They can signal downtrends or uptrends. Whereas, lagging indicators aids in confirming price actions. They're most useful in times of downtrends and uptrends.

-Examples of trend indicators are the ADX and Aroon indicators. The ADX utilizes both negative and positive directional indicators. It can determine the strength of an impending downtrend or uptrend. The scale used is zero to one hundred. If the value is below 20, then the probability of the trend is low. Values above 40 is a sign of a strong trend.

-Aroon indicator, on the other hand, plots the duration of the lowest and highest trading prices. The output data determines the trend's strength and nature. It also helps in predicting when is the emergence of the next trend.

-The OBV is an indicator that relates to trading volume. It encompasses the whole trading volume of a security for a specific period. An OBV with a positive value implies that the asset's price is increasing; a negative value will turn up when the price is decreasing.

-About the RSI and stochastic oscillator

Both the stochastic oscillator and the RSI measures the frequency of the trades for the given security. The index ranges from zero to one hundred. If the value is over seventy, then the asset is being purchased too frequently. A value below thirty indicates that many are selling the asset at a very fast rate.

Typically, RSI is utilized for periods of 2 weeks. This makes it highly liquid. Also, the stochastic oscillator ranges from zero to one hundred and signals frequent purchases at over eighty. Frequent selling is obvious at a value under twenty.

If you trade on margin so that you can resell the security at a higher price at a later date, waiting for the price to reach support provides an opportunity to make money. In the future, you will have to return the money to your broker. Nevertheless, you've already made a profit.

You can also sell at the strength and buy at pullback. A pullback is a reversal of a rising trend. This offers a slim chance to buy at a low price. This is another phrase for "buy low, and sell high." Often, seasoned traders buy assets of any kind when they're being valued at a high price. You can do this at the resistance level or near the peak.

Choosing a Broker, TA Strategy and Trading System

The main focus of this section is to guide you through the process of designing your own trading system. It may not take long to develop one, but testing it and choosing a broker may take some time.

Once you have a trading system and strategy, you know the features, indicators, securities data, and charts you need for technical analysis. Your broker should be able to provide the tools for you. If not, then you can use third-party tools like charting programs and real-time securities scanners.

1. Choose a strategy for your trading style

Do you prefer trading stocks, Forex, or futures? Which do you prefer, long position or short position? There are no two traders out there, so even if you copy the strategies of the most seasoned traders, it isn't guaranteed that it will work for you.

Do you know what's best? You need to devise your own strategy. It may be a modified version of the trading strategy of your favorite trader. Nevertheless, you've made it your own, making it compatible with your personality and capital. Here's how you can do this:

a) Form your market ideology

As a trader, you've to be a reader. That's how you can get through this step. You need to research and research.

Firstly, you must know the indicators that affect your preferred security to trade. Ask yourself, "What are the large entities that can control its value?" "Should you use technical analysis or fundamental analysis?

In this step, avoid get-rich styles. Think about the trading volume and the supply and demand in the market. Your market ideology will help shape the succeeding steps.

b) Choose a market

Your future trading platform must have good offers for trading the security. For example, currency trading involves selling with a quote. If you prefer to trade equities, you need options for choosing penny stocks or blue-chips. The golden rule in this step is to understand your preferred market and your chosen trading platform.

c) Select a time frame

Should you opt for 5-minute time frames or those that an hour-long? Are you suitable for reading daily charts? The answer to these questions is your availability. If you have free time to watch the market like a prowling vulture, then go for hour-long time frames.

Short ones are best suited for those who treat trading as a sideline. If you have a full-time job, you won't be able to commit to hour-long time frames. In this case, you can work with end-of-day charts Either case, make sure that your broker offers or you have access to the charting tools you need.

d) Choose your tools for watching trends

You trade when the asset's price is rising, and you can use a bullish Pin Bar to initiate your trade. Likewise, you won't trade when you see a Gimme Bar.

Rather, the tool is used to confirm whether or not the asset's price is going sideways. It's also utilized to enter the market.

You use tools and programs to watch real-time price statistics and judge market context. Aside from technical indicators, like MAs and MACDs, price movement tools, such as trend lines and swing pivots, can come in handy.

e) Plan your exit trigger

Similar to entering a trade, your exit should also be planned. This is where stop/loss orders would prove to be beneficial. Remember, the market won't be in your favor forever. If you reach a specific amount of loss, you may be able to get out automatically.

f) Define risks

In the next chapter, you'll learn more about electronic trading risks and how to mitigate them.

Once you've planned your exit and entry rules with the use of tools and triggers, you can start working on risk management.

Position sizing can help you reduce risks and improve accuracy. For any trade setup, position size defines the amount of money you'll put into play. For example, if you triple your trade's size, you're also tripling risks. In chapter?, you can learn how to mitigate trading risks.

g) List down your trading rules

You can do this step on paper or with the help of your trusty personal computer. By doing this, you have a firm and robust method that promotes consistency and discipline. By creating a record of your strategy and the rules you have for your style, you can reuse it for other types of trades and be able to refine it with ease.

h) Employ back-testing

Having written your trading rules, you can now proceed to backtesting. To do this, you've to replay market price actions, restudy trends, and record trades manually. Lastly, you need to test your strategy and trades using your chart and past trends.

See and check if you can make a profit with your predictions by playing with your strategy and historical data. Choose a given time frame and start from there.

With your written rules, you can now backtest the strategy. Looking through trades manually is a good method to develop a market instinct, more so than relying on data generators wherein you just input data and have the results on your screen within seconds.

i) Refining your trading strategy

After backtesting, you can have a general idea of the key areas that need improvement. Does your stop/loss order work for your capital? Were your test predictions accurate?

What was the probability of success? Here are tips you can use for this step:

> ➢ Utilize a demo account for your tests and backtests.

> ➢ Review your day trades, whether mock or actual.

> ➢ Adapt your trading plan based on your review.

2. Identify securities

Please keep in mind that not all types of financial securities will be suited to your strategy. In this step, you must ask yourself the following questions:

> ➢ Are my trading rules and system ideal for volatile stocks or stable ones?

> ➢ Can I get all the resources needed for my analysis?

> ➢ Do I have the funds to earn a good amount of profit in each trade?

> ➢ What position will I take?

Different securities also require different parameters. In the aforementioned example, a 15-day and 50-day MA would be suitable.

3. Choosing the right broker

Your chosen broker, platform, and trading account must support your preferred security (e.g., options, stock, futures, Forex, options, etc.). Above all, it must offer the necessary functionalities for tracking and observing selected indicators while minimizing costs and maximizing profits. For the example above, a basic trading account with MAs on candlestick charts would be adequate.

> Foremost, they must be able to provide a demo account.

> Match your style with a broker that charges the least amount of fees

> Don't just compare commission. You must also consider other costs, like service charges and margin interest.

> The broker must be accessible. Also, you need to find out who covers for them if whether or

not they're regulated. Only choose brokers that are regulated.

➢ You may get referrals. Do you know someone who has been a seasoned trader? Why not ask him/her for advice.

➢ Avoid brokers that insist on large investments where they can greatly benefit from. Find out the amount of commissions and how they're determined.

➢ Examine their margin rules and the fees for every transaction. Check for additional fees and charges as well.

➢ Be careful with deep discount brokers. Their discounts may have hidden charges or high fees.

➢ User-friendliness is also another feature to consider. The interface and the responsiveness of the website, as well as the people that run it, must be taken into consideration. When you need help or an inquiry answered, their CS team should be available during trading hours and there must be a section for FAQs and guidelines.

➢ The ease of withdrawals and deposits and the margin requirements are also very important. Reliability is what you need to get your profits fast. How many hours pr days does it for them to process your deposit and payment requests? When it comes to taking your profits away and fulfilling options for getting out of the market, they must be reliable.

➢ If they don't fulfill regulations, they have to answer to regulators. They'll have their license revoked and face fees and criminal charges if they do something to the funds of traders. That's why you need to choose a licensed broker. The US Securities and Exchange Commission (SEC) and the Financial Regulatory Authority (FINRA) are some examples of such governing bodies.

➢ For every broker you review, always consider their reception. Do they have good reviews? Visit websites like brokerchoosers.com and Forexbrokers.com. By doing so, you can have a general idea of the experiences of the majority of their users.

5. Tracking trades and additional tools

Day traders need various functionality levels. What does this mean? For example, you may need a margin account providing access to Level 2 quotes and the feature called "market maker visibility."

You also need additional tools. What are the most important tools in day trading? Here are the tools and services needed for day trading:

> Breaking news software

> Charting app

> Real-time market scanner/market maker

> Scanning software

You may need phone and email alerts. This can come in handy when you're margin trading. As well, you must be vigilant of price movements. Letting an opportunity snuck past under your nose would be an opportunity lost forever.

Lastly, an automated trading system could be beneficial to you too, especially if you need someone or something to execute trades on your behalf.

More Tips and Understanding the Risk Factors

Trading is challenging. That's a fact. Day traders have it harder than investors and swing traders. They need to study the market and the charts almost every day. As a day trader, you need to do your homework thoroughly.

Here are some more pointers that you may benefit from:

> ➤ Backtest your trading strategy. You need to see how your trading style and strategy work. By doing this, you can check the efficacy and accuracy of your predictions with your analysis. Don't cheat. Choose a duration and start and end date, and begin your first trial from there.

> ➤ There's no need to rush. You must consider practicing using a demo account once you're done reading this book and after devising your trading system and plans. After these, log in to your preferred platform and conduct "mock" trades with a practice account.

- ➤ Remember, always be flexible especially when you're margin trading. Brokers can change their policies, so you need to be ready with future requirements.

- ➤ Once you've chosen a broker, go for a trial account first before depositing any money or upgrading to a VIP or premium plan.

- ➤ Warren Buffet, one of Forbe's top 10 richest in the world, said, "start small and expand as you improve."

Using TA and FA for Optimum Strategy

Technical analysis evolved from Dow's stock market theories. TA aims to predict future prices of tradable assets, based on performance and historical prices. Meanwhile, the fundamental analysis considers intrinsic values that could determine price action and the future status of an asset. Both FA and TA use the law of supply and demand to identify trends, profit from them, and understand how the markets work.

Many day traders and investors leverage technical and fundamental analysis when formulating trading decisions. TA can fill in gaps of knowledge that FA can't provide. As well, FA can make the results of TA more accurate and easier to implement. By using both, you can improve long-term risk-adjusted returns. In chapter 6, you can gain more knowledge about trading risks.

Chapter Summary

Many traders analyze stocks and other assets based on their fundamentals, like revenue, industry trends, and valuation. However, such intrinsic values aren't reflected in the price of the asset.

Technical analysis, on the other hand, aims to predict price action by examining past price data and historical trading volume. TA helps both investors and speculators diminish the gap between market price and intrinsic value through leveraging trading strategies, such as behavioral economics and statistical analysis.

At its core, TA guides traders to what may happen using past data. For decision-making, most speculators use both fundamental and technical analysis.

Step 5: Knowing More About Day Trading

There are two types of professional traders: hedgers and speculators. Hedgers find protection against price changes. Speculators look to gain profit from price movements--the action of a security's price plotted overtime. Price changes are the basis for all types of technical analysis used in electronic trading. Short-term traders, such as the day traders, rely heavily on price action.

The trends and formations extrapolated from historical data, through analysis, help in formulating successful trading decisions. Hedgers, unlike speculators, make their trading (buy and sell) choices as insurance. Speculators choose their positions to make a profit, offsetting their exposure in other markets.

The Role of Day Trading

To clarify everything that has been said, take a food-processing company for example. The skilled worker, who raises the ingredients required in manufacturing, such as corn and meat, purchases future contracts on those ingredients.

By doing that, if prices go up, the prospected profits of the organization decrease. This could be a compromise to the company. The farmer, on the other hand, benefits if prices increase and suffer if the selling price decrease.

To protect against that, the farmer can sell futures on his commodities. What are futures? Futures are financial contracts. These contracts obligate buyers to buy assets in advance or oblige sellers to sell assets.

Future contracts have predetermined prices and future dates. Futures hedges the price action of underlying assets. This move helps prevent losses from unfavorable price actions. In the example above, the buyer is the company and the farmer is the seller.

The farmer can sell futures on his commodities to protect himself against any price decline. His futures position on the trade will only make money if the price decrease, as it offsets the decrease of prices of his products. Also, with future contracts, he will lose money because of the contracts, but his profits from his harvest offset the loss.

Commodity markets were established to help farmers and agriculturists find buyers and manage risks. The bond and stock markets, in contrast, create incentives for investors and buyers to finance their companies. Speculation, the act of trading that has a high chance of losing value, but also has a high probability for a significant gain is present in all of these markets. Speculation is also common in Forex, stocks, cryptocurrency, options, and other electronic markets.

Day traders are speculators. They're sophisticated individuals who buy assets for short periods. They employ trading strategies to make profits from price changes. Like hedgers, they are important to markets because they promote liquidity and keep the value of assets active.

Speculators day trade to make money from the current status of markets. Managing risks by allocating money using stop and limit orders, they don't take long positions. Their orders close out as soon as set price levels are reached.

Unlike hedgers, day traders don't manage their risks by offsetting positions. Rather, they employ techniques and strategies that can limit losses. This will be discussed more in the succeeding sections. For example, they employ money management tactics and limit or stop orders. Any electronic market has hedgers and speculators trading in them.

By knowing the various participants and their loss and profit expectations, you can manage day trading and stir away from the turmoils it brings. This is very important since you can only make money from the losses of others in zero-sum markets.

The Zero-sum Markets

The zero-sum markets have as many winners as losers. Stocks, Forex, futures, and options are prominent with day traders. In chapter 8, day trading with the said securities will be further discussed. In such markets, when one makes a profit, someones loses money. That's one notable element in zero-sum markets.

Zero-sum is a situation in game theory, wherein one's gain is equivalent to another's loss. The net equal in benefit or wealth is zero. In trading, futures and options are examples of zero-sum games, excluding the cost of the transaction. As a whole, there's no net loss or net gain.

What does that mean for day traders? Day trading is like a zero-sum game. Most day traders in such markets are also hedgers. They're contented with taking small losses to lower risks in trading, preventing big losses. In specific market conditions, speculators, which are mostly day traders, have a profit advantage. Still, they shouldn't count on those "advantages" at all times.

Who loses and wins in such markets? There are times that the winner depends on luck. But over the long run, the winners are disciplined traders. The winners in zero-sum markets are those who have a trading plan. Initial losses could just be a part of their strategy.

Some sell a lot to increase the asset's value and reach the ceiling price for the day. That's just one type of tricky trading strategy. Doesn't that peak your interest?

Disciplined traders employ strategies, make use of analyses, set limits, and stick to those limits. They trade based on data rather than emotions, such as greed, fear, and hope. In the next chapter, you'll learn more about trading psychology and the traits needed to develop by traders.

The stock market, however, is not a zero-sum market, although many speculators trade here. As long as the economy improves, the value of the stocks increase. At the end of the day, the number of winners in stock markets is greater than in zero-sum markets. If you know how profits are divided in your preferred market, you will be aware of the risks and what other participants face.

Electronic trading is all about rewards and risks. You don't want others to be making money from your losses. You may be doing what you like, but you will go nowhere if you keep losing.

Closing Your Positions Every Trading Day's End

Day traders start their day fresh because they finish each one with a new beginning--a clean slate. This daily routine decreases risks and forces discipline into people. When there's a possibility for profit, you shouldn't just sit around and watch others take the opportunities. You must refrain from keeping losses longer than one day and always take your profits at the end of each trading day since winning positions can turn into losing positions overnight.

Doing those decreases risks, and that discipline is important for speculators and day traders. When engaging in day trading, the market doesn't care about your identity or your preferences. You own your time, yet you don't have a boss who can cut you a little slack. You have no coworker who can serve as your substitute, unless you opt for automatic trading or have hired someone to watch the market for you. And lastly, you don't have a client who can drop you hints. Unless you have set rules for yourself and a guide for your trading decisions, you'll be the prey of the

Four Horsemen of Trading Ruin--greed, doubt, fear, and hope.

How to discipline yourself? Firstly, you must develop a trading plan and business plan. These two should be different from each other, and they must reflect your personality and goals. After the first step, you've to set your work hours and trading days. These steps are covered in chapter 5.

While thinking about your options, you must test your trading system. This can help you create an effective trading system perfect for your lifestyle and capabilities. By doing so, you can put your strategies and plans into action. Simply put, you need to prepare and create a plan. Whether you're building a new chicken coop, joining a triathlon, or engaging in day trading, those two steps are the basic strategy of winners.

Exploring the Different Kinds of Trading Markets

As trading innovation continues and advents in technology increase, the world of electronic trading keeps expanding, and more financial instruments can be used. Even commodities markers are stealing each other's market share. A company, entity, or product controls the portion of a market.

For example, an individual who needs to purchase gold physically or by a futures contract can now buy an exchange-traded fund (ETF) so that he or she can participate in the price movement of gold.

Since similar scenarios also apply to stocks, commodities, currencies, and other securities, online traders can fine-tune their strategies for different circumstances, like during day- or swing trading.

-What are the financial markets?

Financial and trading markets refer to any market where securities trading occurs. This includes derivatives, Forex, bonds, and stocks. Financial markets are integral to the effective operation of capitalist nations. They create liquidity and allocate resources for entrepreneurs and businesses.

The marketplaces facilitate the act of trading for both sellers and buyers. Through electronic trading, they can buy and sell specific securities, which are discussed below, online.

The financial markets allow for the trade of securities products. These offer a return for the people (the traders and investors) who have funds to purchase on a brokerage platform. The buyers, especially the day traders, resell the securities for profit.

For example, the stock market is a type of financial market. Through online brokers and similar platforms, you can trade national and international stocks. However, some local stocks are only available for trading in national financial organizations. In Japan, IC Markets and XTB Online Trading allows for the trading of national-level public shares.

Financial markets are formed by trading many types of financial instruments, which include derivatives, currencies, bonds, and equities. These marketplaces rely heavily on data transparency to ensure that the prices inside the market are appropriate.

The intrinsic value of the securities, like gold, doesn't indicate their market prices. This is because they're also affected by taxes and other macroeconomic factors.

Some markets have little activity. They're small compared to others, such as local stock exchanges. FirstMetroSec in the Philippines is an example of a local stock exchange.

In contrast, the NASDAQ and NYSE experience millions of trades daily and trillions of dollars circulate on these markets, every 24 hours. The equity market or the stock market allows hedgers, investors, and speculators to publicly sell shares of companies they've invested in.

In primary stock markets, new stocks can be issued. Newly-issued stocks are referred to as initial public offers (IPOs). Subsequent stock tradings can also be conducted in secondary markets. This is where investors trade securities that are already known.

The Different Trading Markets

Depending on your experience, you may even be aware of the trading or investment mediums that are available to you with just one click. Even when avoiding illiquid and abstract markets, speculators can find transactions within various markets that are within their budget. Here are the most notable markets and exchanges where you can day trade.

-OTC markets

Over-the-counter markets are decentralized. This means that they don't have physical locations. And, securities trading is conducted online, or electronically. Online, participants in the market include traders and investors.

In the next sections, you will learn how to choose the right platform and method of trading suitable for you. Will you participate in OTC markets? Do you prefer brokers and brokerage platforms?

An OTC market can handle the exchanges of stocks that aren't listed on the NYSE and American Stock Exchange. Generally, financial organizations and entities that trade in OTC and other primary markets require fewer fees and less regulation than secondary markets, which is also called aftermarket in which traders and investors trade financial securities they already own.

Here are more pros and cons of trading in OTC markets:

Pros

> High volatility

> The ability to stay ahead of inflation

> Unmatched liquidity

> Flexibility for beginners

> Growth opportunities

Cons

> Sudden market crashes

> Subjection to higher risks

-Stock Market

The stock market is the collection of exchanges and platforms where daily activities of issuance and trading of shares of publicly-held companies occur. These financial activities are executed through OTC marketplaces, brokerage platforms, and institutionalized formal exchanges.

Stock markets, whether they have a physical location or none, operate following set regulations. In any country, region, or state that allows stocks and securities trading, there could be multiple venues for stock and Forex trading. The NASDAQ and NYSE are two of the world's largest securities exchange with physical locations. Major brokerage platforms all offer stock trading.

While the terms stock exchange and stock market can be used interchangeably, the former is just a subset of the latter. If you say you trade in the stock market, this means you trade equities/shares on a stock exchange that is part of the stock market.

The most notable stock exchanges in the world include the NASDAQ, NYSE, and CBOE, or the Chicago Board Options Exchange. These leading national stock exchanges, along with smaller exchanges existing within the country, comprises the US stock market.

A bourse, securities exchange, or stock is a facility or platform where traders and stockbrokers can trade securities, including bonds and shares of stocks. Some also issue issues and allow for the redemption of securities, capital events, and financial instruments as well as the payment of income and dividends. Dividends are the profit you get from your investments in common shares.

Although most trades in the markets involve public shares, ETF, bonds, and currency trades also transpire in stock markets. The same can be said in Forex markets. This is also true for the US stock markets.

-Bond Markets

What's a bond? A bond is a security in which an investor loans a specific amount of money for a defined period at a pre-established interest rate. Bonds are agreements between the borrower and the lender containing the details of the contract\deal, including the details of the loan and its subsequent payments.

Sovereign governments, as well as states, and municipalities, can issue bonds. The issuance could be for financing operations and projects. The bond market is also referred to as the credit, debit, and fixed-income markets. It involves trades of securities like bills and notes issued by the US Treasury.

How to trade bonds? Understanding bond trading and bond markets are important to proper day trading. The bond market is bigger than the stock market and bond trading occurs thousands, if not millions, of times per day.

When speculators trade bonds, they specify the different types of bonds they're trading. In turn, this sets the credit price in the economy. This is why the bond market affects many economies around the world, both negatively and positively.

Unlike stocks, bonds can be traded anywhere that a seller and buyer can conduct a transaction. There is no exchange or central place for bond trading. In fact, this market is a type of over-the-counter market. Nevertheless, convertible bonds, like bond options and bond futures, are traded on formal exchanges, including online brokerage platforms. An in-depth discussion of this topic is included in the last chapter of this book.

-The ETF Market

Funds that represent multiple sectors, industries, and commodities are involved in ETF markets. Like stocks, you can trade such securities daily or hoard them in your account for swing trading.

-The Forex Market

Also known as the currency market, the Forex market is the largest in the world. It's also the most liquid and has accounted for billions of trades per day. In 2010, it has accounted for $3 trillion of daily trading. Although it hasn't existed a century ago, it's where the majority of day-traders buy and sell securities.

Foreign exchange markets facilitate the trades of one currency for another. Even though daily currency trades can be also conducted electronically, stock trading is different from Forex trading. Currencies are traded in pairs, while stocks are traded in units.

-The Options Market

The options market is a marketplace that enables participants to take positions in the derivative of an asset\security. Hence, the option--a contract that enables an investor to trade a financial instrument like an index or ETF at a set price over a certain period--is based on specific securities. The value of options and other inputs changes with the value, or the lack of, that the asset in question provides.

-CFDs

CFD stands for Contract for Difference. This is an arrangement made in derivatives trades, wherein the differences in the given settlement between the first and last trade prices are settled by cash. This is a type of option whereby physical delivery of the security or asset isn't required. The settlement leads to a cash payment, rather than settling in bonds, stocks, or commodities.

A settlement, in finance and trading, is a business process, by which securities or interests in securities are physically delivered to fulfill contractual obligations. These days, settlements typically take place in central securities depositories (CSDs).

A CSD is a financial organization that holds securities like shares or stocks in dematerialized or certificated form. Through a CSD, ownership of a financial security can be transferred. This is executed with a book entry, instead of the transfer of physical certificates. This allows brokers, electronic platforms, and financial organizations to hold securities at a single location. This makes them available for electronic clearing and settlement.

This option type avoids expenses for transaction and transport fees. CFDs don't expire. The CFD market is in fact a hybrid of the Forex, stock, and options market.

Like other markets, the CFD market is accessible anywhere that has an internet connection. All of them have disadvantages and advantages. For this reason, most traders focus on only one type of security to trade. They are afraid to transact in other markets aside from what suits their personality best. This is mainly due to a lack of knowledge.

However, the successful ones do otherwise. Given their trading style, they primarily take advantage of one market and hedge or trade on another as a sideline.

What's the Best Market for You?

You must consider your location, financial resources, and day trading style when choosing which market to participate in. To help you decide on things like that is one of the purposes of this book. It's integral to be aware of other alternatives so that you can easily fine-tune your trades and get profitable results. For a more detailed discussion of this topic, please refer to the next section, chapter 7, and chapter 8.

Alternative Markets for Aspiring Day Traders

Since the 2000 stock market crash, the number of turnovers in the Forex market has increased. In investing, turnover is the percentage of a financial portfolio sold in a specific year or month. A fast turnover rate generates high commissions for transactions placed by a broker.

That implies an increase in the number of new-day traders in the CFD and Forex markets. The greatest lure by brokers is their low initial deposits. Most well-refuted online brokers only require at least $100 to open an account and start trading Forex and stocks.

In the Forex market, the trader exchanges one currency for another. The low commission may sound nice, but in such platforms, a spread must be paid in every transaction.

The bottom line is, you must be aware that multiple markets are out there. Even though it isn't advisable to participate in all of them due to restrictions and time limitations, the use of a combination of markets or the fine-tuning of trading strategies can positively impact results.

For some traders, they need to change markets from time to time since their trading success depends on that. In contrast, entering two or more markets can provide advantages such as risk reduction, capital outlays, and changes in cost. Just remember that becoming familiar with the markets provides more opportunities and increased profits and reduced costs.

-The Stock Exchanges

What's a stock exchange? Stock exchanges are physical and virtual places where stocks can be traded. An exchange of this type is highly regulated, despite being dominated by electronic trading.

How to Day Trade

"Betting against the trend" is an example of a trading strategy. This is also called contrarian investing and is used by many stock traders, including those that manipulate price movements and market volatility. If the market or a stock experiences a downtrend, you buy and trade against the market. You speculate that going up the trend will favor you and your capital.

Highly experienced traders use this strategy. They fully understand the market, and they have profited many times from doing the opposite of what the majority does. Betting against the trend is risky, but it offers high profits.

For example, if the stock market you're participating in is currently bullish, you hedge and take long positions. If you're in a bear market and you take long positions, you're also going against the trend. Your trading success depends on the factors affecting the trend. You need careful and diligent research before employing this money-making tactic.

By simply buying low, you aren't exactly trading in the said fashion. However, it could result in that if effectively done. For example, when day traders predict that a stock will fall low, they may borrow shares and sell them for the purpose of trading at low prices. When they prefer day trading, they will take short positions.

-Short Trades

Taking short positions can be confusing to most traders. In reality, we need to buy something for us to sell it. In short trades, day traders sell securities before purchasing them. They do this to make a profit from a price decrease. Their trade will only generate profits if the amount they borrowed is lower than the selling price of the asset. In financial markets, you can buy and then sell, or sell and then buy.

Day traders utilize the words short and sell interchangeably. Likewise, some programs and trading platforms have a trading button marked short or sell. The use of the word "short" in the sentence "I am short apple" indicates that you're in a short position in Apple stock.

To reiterate, day traders who like taking short positions often say "go short" or "going short." This indicates their interest in taking a short position in a specific asset. Similar to the example in chapter 2, if you go short on 1,000 shares of YYY stock at $9, you receive $9,000 in your account upon completion of the trade. If you can buy 1,000 shares of stock YYY at $10.60 per share, you will have to pay $10,600. If you resell all your purchased shares at $11,000, you receive $11,000 by going short. Hence, your profit will be $400, less commissions.

If the value of stock increases and if you repurchase 1,000 shares at $9.20, then you've to pay $9,200 for the shares. In this situation, you lose $200 aside from the commission.

-Can You Take a Short Position in any Market?

Traders can go short in most financial markets, In the Forex and Futures market, you can always go short. Most public stocks are shortable. The majority of stocks are like this, but not all of them.

In 2010, the SEC imposed an alternative uptick rule. This rule prevents short selling from decreasing the value of a particular stock if its share price has dropped by 10% in just one day.

In margin trading, your broker needs to borrow the shares from an individual or entity that owns the shares. If he can't borrow for you, you can't short the stock. New stocks in the exchange, which are called IPOs, or initial public offerings, aren't shortable.

Better Understanding Stocks and Shares

In financial markets, the distinction between shares and stocks is blurry. As a rule, you can use both words interchangeably when referring to financial equity. This includes securities denoting ownership in a company.

In the olden days of paper transactions, such securities are referred to as "stock certificates." Today, the difference between the two depends on syntax and the context of their usage.

Here are some key points for better understanding:

> ➢ For all purposes and intents, shares and stocks can refer to the same thing.

➤ The distinction is only considered for legal or financial accuracy. That's why traders and investors use the words interchangeably.

➤ Specifically, to invest in the shares of a public company's stocks, a trading account is required.

➤ Of the two, "stocks" is commonly used, and "shares" has a very specific meaning. The former refers to a slice of ownership of a public company. On the other hand, "shares" describe the ownership of a particular company.

➤ Take note that you can own shares of various financial instruments (e.g. ETFs, mutual funds, limited partnerships, etc.) In contrast, stocks refer to corporate equities. These are public shares that can be traded on stock exchanges.

➤ What's a preferred stock? Now, two types of equity exist. They are preferred stock and common stock. Preferred shares or preferred stock entitles holders to a fixed dividend. The dividends are paid out to stockholders before the issuance of common stock dividends.

Getting Started

In financial markets, day-traded securities are bought and sold within a single day. That's the maxim of day-trading. Rather than hoarding assets for weeks or months, speculators like day traders purchase securities, such as stocks or Forex, hoping that the value rises within that same day. They take short positions before the day ends and make sure that another market participant will purchase their asset. To get started with day trading, please follow the step-by-step guide below:

1) Budgeting

This is the very first phase and it is subdivided into three phases:

a) Decide your capital.

b) Create a trading account.

c) Read the rules and regulations and make sure to follow them to the fullest and meet all requirements before trading.

d) Deposit your preferred amount or at least the minimum capital required by the broker.

2) Trading through your broker.

As mentioned earlier, it's best to evaluate various brokers and brokerage platforms. If you prefer to request the brokers to make the trades for you, you must tell him/her your preferences, including rules you've set for your strategies and what order will you opt for. You also need to always clarify how much you'll trade.

Lastly, for this step, contact the firm with inquiries about their business practices. Before depositing any amount, don't hesitate to ask questions directly. Inquire about fees, liquidity, and withdrawals. Remember, once you make profits, you will want to withdraw your money. Their modes of payment should be flexible and reliable. PayPal, TransferWise, and Western Union are well-refuted and trusted online payment systems.

3) Strategizing your online trades

As a beginner trader, avoid trading a significant chunk of your capital. Limit each trade to 1 to 2%

of it. If you start by investing 10% or more of your funds, you may exhaust the money you've set aside for trading. For example, if you deposited $1,000 to your account, then it's advised that your first trades should only cost $10 to $20. Likewise, if you start with $15,000, then each of your trades must only amount to $150 to $300 or lesser.

Remember Warren Buffet's words "Start small, and expand as you grow."

The "scalping" method is a favorite of many beginners and professional traders. It allows for quick profits, albeit small.

For this strategy to work, you need to sell your purchased securities, as soon as you can make a profit from them. For example, if you purchased 20 shares of stock XXX at $2 per share, and 15 minutes later, the value increased to $2.05 per share, then you can make a quick, small profit. In the scenario above, you have made a dollar in 15 minutes. The higher the number of units of your chosen security you purchase, the higher your profit will be.

The so-called "momentum strategy" involves fundamental analysis and following breaking news about given stocks. It promotes day-trading on 1 to 2 stocks that will do well for the day. For example, if gaming stocks may thrive in the coming week. Purchase 10 to 20 shares of stocks from well-rooted tech companies in the industry. But, before you do that, make sure that that stock is volatile and has been doing well in the long run. Consider using TA or FA to make value and effective trades. When one or more of the assets wherein you've invested has risen by 20 to 30%, sell your shares/units of the security at high point or near the resistance level.

However, if the value keeps rising, always be vigilant of sudden significant reversals. If the market is gradually entering a bear market, but the asset remains volatile, then take advantage of mini trends. Sell high, and buy low. If the price will likely hit an all-time bottom soon, get out of the market.

4) Diversify your financial portfolio and improve your trades

Day trading is a great way to diversify markets and improve your financial portfolio. You can invest in a market through swing trading while you're speculating on another. If you have a small capital, you can further subdivide it for two purposes:

➢ Study the markets

➢ Gauge which is the perfect fit for you

Each tradable security offers different opportunities for making a profit. With the data you've gathered through observation and analysis, you can decide, with good judgment, where you can make lots of profits.

Step 6: Speculating in the Forex Market

Does keeping your impulses in check the best way to trade Forex? Like in other markets, do you need a trading strategy to win big in foreign exchanges? What's the best way to read Forex charts? If you're still a beginner in this field, the first trades can be overwhelming

Day trading in the Forex market is harder than speculating in the stocks market. There are a lot of terms to learn before you can day trade effectively! Nevertheless, investing your time and money in the world's largest market can bring in high profits.

Forex trading is also known as currency trading. It's all about profits, rates, trends, and losses. Your losses will be dependent on factors, failed predictions, and trading strategy. Nevertheless, if you employ an effective trading system in every attempt to make money in the market, you can easily gain profits and avoid losses.

In chapter 4, you've learned how to develop a winning trading system. This chapter is all about the world of Forex trading. It holds everything you need to know for day trading currencies.

What's Waiting for You in this Market?

With the advent of IoT (Internet of Things) and the World Wide Web, millions of people around the world, including investors, retirees, solo parents, and young adults are discovering the advantages of Forex Trading. To most of them, trading in Forex markets is their livelihood. Their profits are more than enough to cover their living expenses.

Some have even made a fortune out of Forex trading. With the Foreign exchange market, you can trade for just $20 or $100, but this depends on your broker. You can also leverage for high returns or borrow from a financer.

Forex, or FX, trading is also referred to as currency trading. The Forex market, as a whole, is a decentralized global market, in which many of the world's currencies are traded on a daily basis. It's the largest and most liquid market in the world.

On average, the Forex market's daily trading volume exceeds $5 trillion. Even if all the stock and bond markets are combined, they won't come close to the trading volume in the currency market.

Have you gone abroad? If someone has sent you money from abroad, you may have already made a Forex trade. For instance, you went to Seoul, Korea, and you converted your USD to KRW (Korean Won). The foreign exchange rate between the two aforementioned currencies determines how much KRW you would've gotten with your dollars.

The exchange of a pair, which involves two currencies, is based on the supply and demand in the market. The exchange rates fluctuate continuously. This is because they're affected by many factors, such as terms of trade, fluctuation rates, and political stability and performance.

To reiterate, foreign exchange is quite similar to the stock market. Like stocks, you can trade currencies based on estimates.

The major difference between the two is the fact that you're simultaneously buying one currency and selling another in Forex trading. This is different from stock trading. You either sell your shares or buy more stocks.

Also, you can easily average up or down with Forex. Averaging up in the currency market is exactly the opposite of averaging down in stock trading. This remains true for the fact that when your trades go in your favor, the best move is to add more positions. In the later sections of this chapter, you'll learn more about this strategy.

In May 2020, Japan devalued its currency to attract more foreign investors and businessmen. If you think that this trend will last for a long time, like a few weeks or several months, then easy opportunities for Forex trading will definitely arise. In this situation, you can make profitable trades by selling the JPY (Japanese Yen) against the Euro, US dollar, or Australian dollar.

The more the JPY devalues against your preferred currency, the higher your profits will be. If the JPY devalues while you're position is "open," then you'll lose money. In this case, the best position is to "close" your position within the day.

The example above contains several technical terms. What's devaluation? How can this affect exchange rates? What's a currency pair?

How can indicators and economic factors affect the volatility of the Forex market? If you don't know the essential terms in this trade, barriers will face you when trading Forex. This chapter can teach you the principles behind Forex trading, as well as everything there is to know to make it big in this market.

The True Nature of the Forex Market

The FX market trades 24 hours a day and 5 days a week. Greatest volatility transpires during market overlap. This happens when one offers to purchase a security at a high price and sell at a lower price than the highest bid.

currency markets, traders, as well as investors, can exit and enter trades during global business days.

Three trading sessions--Asia, London, and New York--divide the Forex market. This allows you to choose a trading time according to their schedules. Currency trading transpires over the counter. When a region's business hours close, another region will open theirs.

At specific times of the day, the volume of the asset being traded could become high. This depends on the currency pair. Traders can make large profits during times of high liquidity, like the Asian session, New York session, and London session. Volatility is often high during such times and spreads are lower.

In general, traders trade during the London and New York session, and every overlap. Forex traders don't need to observe the market 24 hours a day. They can take advantage of the currency market by trading when the market is highly liquid. A solid and proven trading strategy should also be utilized.

Here are some key tips when day trading in the currency market:

-Watch out for the holidays

You must take note of every holiday in every region. If the USA has a holiday, then the USD market won't be that liquid during that time. Although the FX market doesn't cease, some brokers and platforms are unavailable during public holidays.

-Use different strategies for different trading sessions

Every FX session has various characteristics, which are detailed in chapter 5. Hence, you must adopt a suitable trading strategy. During low liquidity, you can employ range-bound strategies. What's this?

A range-bound strategy is a method wherein traders purchase a given security at a support level and take a short position at the resistance level. Traders typically utilize this trading strategy along with technical indicators like volume to increase their probability of success.

For example, a trader might have noticed that the given security is starting to generate a price channel. This transpires when the price oscillates between two parallel lines, whether they are descending, ascending, or horizontal. You can sell when the value nears the channel's upper trend and take a long position when the lower trendline is being tested.

In the given scenario, the channel in late-August and early-September formed initial peaks. The trader might have placed short and long trades in reference to the trendlines. His market activities totaled two long trades and four short trades.

The asset's breakout from the upper resistance level indicates the end to the trading following a range-bound strategy.

-The currency pairs

There are many currency pairs. All in all, there are 180 currencies that are circulating throughout the world. Some are considered "minor," "major," and "exotic." The major pairs include:

> USD/CHF

> GBP/JPY

> EUR/JPY

> GBP/USD

- ➢ USD/JPY

- ➢ EUR/USD

Every day, they're traded in high volumes. This implies that transactions involving the aforementioned currency pairs offer low costs and reduced spreads for traders.

The Fundamentals of Forex Trading

Forex is a portmanteau of foreign currency and exchange. Forex is the act or process of converting a currency to another.

Therefore, you trade currencies whenever you convert your dollars into another country's currency. According to the BIS (the Bank of International Settlements, roughly $5 trillion is the daily trading volume in the Forex market.

The market establishes the rates for currencies around the world. In trading, the "exchange rate" is the figure at which a specific currency can be traded into another.

The Forex rate of a currency is its value. Foreign exchange is the conversion of one currency into another at a rate known as "the foreign exchange rate." This constantly fluctuates, since the market forces of supply and demand drive the rates for all currencies in the world.

For example, the exchange rate of 100 JPY to 1 USD implies that ¥100 is equivalent to $1. Similarly, 1$ can be exchanged for ¥100. In this case, you can say that the value of 1 USD against the JPY is ¥100. Equivalently, the value of 1 JPY relative to 1 USD is $1/100.

The Forex market determines the exchange rates, which include Foreign and interbank exchange rates. The term "interbank rate" can also refer to the Foreign exchange rates. To reiterate, the market is open 24 hours a day Mondays to Fridays.

Currencies are traded in pairs. What's this? A pair is a quote for two different currencies in a foreign exchange. When you order a currency pair, the first listed currency (the base) is purchased. The quote (the second currency) is sold. In the JPY/USD pair, the Japanese Yen is the base and the USD is the quote.

To date, the EUR\USD currency pair is the most liquid in the whole world. In trading, liquidity refers to how one can quickly convert a specific currency, held in an electronic platform, into hard cash. Liquid assets include cash, checkable account, and savings account.

With regards to the aforementioned currency pair, you can convert your funds into money because of the liquidity of the pair. Since it's the most liquid pair, many are trading and converting the EUR into USD, around the world. Aside from conventional modes of payments, you may be able to withdraw your money in banks or money remittance centers.

In foreign exchanges, the spot exchange FX rate is the current rate of exchange of a currency pair. The forward exchange rate, on the other hand, is the exchange rate in contract for the payment for a currency date at a predetermined date. This is usually set 30, 90, or 180 days in the future.

The market determines the rate of every currency being traded in the exchange. As well, all aspects of trading and converting currencies are determined at current (spot) prices.

The major participants in this exchange are international banks and large financial centers. Day and night, except for Saturdays and Sundays, these financial organizations serve as mediums between millions of traders.

What's a Forex Market?

The Forex market has different levels, and it involves banking institutions. These are corporations, intermediaries of economic systems. Exchange rates are based on the trades and trading volume in the market. In the following sections, you can learn more about the law of supply and demand.

Wherever entities or parties engage in currency exchange, that space, whether physical or virtual, is a market. Hence, a Forex market is just one of the many systems and institutions whereby people can exchange currencies. Brokers, eToro and Ameritrade, run online Forex markets. All Forex markets rely on buyers, sellers, and financial institutions, which are considered "intermediaries."

In Forex markets, brokers and investors can facilitate trades. Although speculators need to adhere to rules and policies in every platform, brokers have streamlined the process of Forex trading, over the years. Specifically, traders must follow proper quoting, competitive pricing, and platform registration.

Things You Need to Know Before Trading Currencies: Pips and Lots

Behind the scenes, banks rely on financial organizations when transacting in the Forex market. These firms are called "dealers." They involve in large currency trades. Most dealers are local, rural, or national banks.

Such organizations operate behind the scenes operate behind-the-scenes and are referred to as the interbank markets. Sometimes, insurance companies and financial firms are also involved.

Trades between two dealers are often large. Each transaction may involve millions of US dollars.

Forex markets serve as a medium for both trades and investments. Currency conversion is one of their core features. Online brokerage platforms, for example, allows US startups to import products from European Union member states. With Forex markets, business owners that reside in foreign countries can buy goods from EU members in EUR.

-Open position

As the term implies, this is an established trade that has yet to become close with another party's trade. An open position can exist after a short position or a long position. Be that as it may, the position will remain open until there's an opposing trade.

An open position is any trade that a market participant has established; An opposing trade can exist after a buy position or sell position. Be that as it may, the position stays open until an opposing trade transpires.

-What Are Currency Pairs

Foreign exchanges mainly hold currency pair trading. Their names combine the two currencies being traded. To reiterate, the base currency is the first currency. It's the one appearing in the pair quotation and then followed by the quote currency. This determines the value of the base or "the first" currency.

In the Forex market, the unit prices of currencies are represented by currency pairs. The base currency (transaction currency) is the 1st currency in the quotation. The second one is the counter or quote currency.

For accounting reasons, a financial organization can use the base currency and the domestic currency to represent all losses and profits. Fundamentally, it represents the total amount of the quote currency being traded. It represents how much of the quote of to acquire one unit of the base.

For instance, if you're looking at the JPY/USD pair, the Japanese Yen is the base and the US dollar is the quote. The International Organization for Standardization (ISO) set the abbreviations utilized for currency trading. The standard ISO 4217 provides the codes. Three letters represent each currency, as in the example of the JPY, CAD, and USD.

The currencies comprising a pair are commonly separated with a slash (/). You can replace the slash with a dash or period. The major codes for currencies include EUR for the euro, the HUSD for the US dollar, the GBP for the British pound, JPY for the Japanese yen. The AUD stands for the Australian dollar, while CAD represents the Canadian dollar.

The Different Parts of a Currency Pair

Currency pairs are written as XXX/YYY or just XXXYYY. In this example, XXX is the base and YYY is the quote. Examples of this format are EURCHF, EURNZD, GBPJPY, etc.

When an exchange rate is added, the pairs indicate how much of the transaction currency is required to purchase one unit of the first currency. For example, the currency pair EUR/USD = 1.26 implies that 1 euro is equivalent to 1.26 USD. This means that you need to pay 1.26 USD to acquire 1 EUR. The quotation is read in the same way when selling the base. Conversely, if you want to sell 1 EUR, you will get 1.26 USD for it.

The reason for this format is because investors and speculators simultaneously buy and sell currencies. For instance, when you buy USD/EUR, this means that you're buying USD and selling EUR at that moment.

Traders, specifically day traders, buy a pair if they predict that the value of the first currency will increase against the quote. Contrastingly, they sell the currency pair if they see that the base will lose value and that the exchange rate for the quote will increase.

What's a Position in Currency Trading?

A position in foreign exchanges is the amount of funds/currency a trader/entity owns in a brokerage platform. Like in stock exchanges, the terms short and long positions are also used in currency trading. Each Forex position has 3 characteristics:

➢ The size of the trade

➢ The direction (short or long)

➢ The underlying currency pair

Traders, as well as entities, can take positions in various currency pairs, such as EUR/JPY or AUD/USD. The position size depends on the margin requirements and the trader's account equity. This refers to the total funds in the trader's account. Equity is their balance plus or minus the loss or profit from open positions.

The margin requirement is the percentage of marginal assets that a trader must pay for with his funds or cash. When he holds the security purchased on margin, the minimum margin at Firstrade for the majority of stocks is lowered to 30%.

Bonds, stocks, futures, and similar assets are marginable securities. This means that the said securities can be traded on margin. Margin trading alludes to trading on money borrowed from a broker to substantially increase market exposure. When engaging in a margin trade, the broker lends a specific amount of money. The loan amount depends on the leverage ratio utilized. (What's this?) A small portion of the trading account is allocated as collateral. The collateral is the margin for that trade.

The act involves purchasing a security where the buyer pays a percentage of the asset's total value. He then has to borrow the rest from the broker. The broker acts as the lender and the securities or funds in the trading account serve as the collateral.

A loan pays for the securities traded on margin, and a broker, brokerage platform, or financial institution facilitates and lends the money for the trade.

Simply put, margin is the amount of funds that the broker will lend to the trader. To calculate margin, subtract the value of securities in the trader's account and the loan amount. Hence, buying on margin is the practice of borrowing money to purchase securities.

Purchasing securities with margin is like using physical assets (e.g. machinery, properties, and other physical properties) as collateral for a bank loan. In trading, the collateralized loan comes with a periodic interest rate. The investor/trader must pay this.

The trader in question is using the leverage or the borrowed money. Hence, both gains and losses are magnified. If the trader can make high profits from a trade, then margin trading is advantageous.

When everything is taken into account, traders can take positions in various currency pairs, as long as they have the funds for it or they can engage in a margin trade. To reiterate, the position size relies on the trader's margin requirements and account equity. The appropriate amount of leverage is important in day trading and trading on margin.

-About Leverage

What's leverage? How much leverage should I use? These are common questions that beginner traders ask.

In trading, leverage is the usage of a loan or borrowed funds to increase one's position size over their trading account's limit. Specifically, Forex traders use leveraging to gain profits from small price movements. Be that as it may, leverage in trading can amplify both losses and profits.

For instance, if you take a loan to buy a house, you're leveraging your balance sheet. The balance sheet shows investors the liabilities and assets owned by the trader. It summarizes what is left when the two are put together. The equation involves the individual's net worth, book value, and shareholder equity.

If you buy a $100,000 house, but you don't have enough savings or on-hand cash, you may have to down 20% of the total price of the property, and then, make regular payments to the seller or bank. In this example, you use your $20,000 cash to control a large asset. With the leverage and existing savings, one can control a large asset.

In the stock market, margin accounts enable traders to leverage their purchases by 2 factors. For example, if you deposit $40,000 into a margin account, then you can control an asset worth no more than $80,000.

-Margin Trading Tutorial

Foremost, margin trading requires a margin account. Based on its definition, this is different from a "trading cash account." The latter is a standard account that beginners can open when they first start trading.

In contrast to a margin account, a normal trading account, or cash account, requires market participants to fund a trade fully before the actual execution. When utilizing cash accounts, debt or margin is unneeded. The trader can't lose more than the funds in his account.

A cash account is different from a margin account. And, some differences exist between the loans a trader can receive for margin trading.

The securities that can exist in a margin account are as follows:

- ➤ Stocks

- ➤ Bonds

- ➢ Futures

- ➢ Options

- ➢ Cryptocurrencies

- ➢ Forex

If one fails to meet the requirements of a margin call, the broker can sell off investments until the equity ratio is restored. This maintenance requirement differs from one broker to another.

The maintenance requirement is the amount you can borrow for every dollar you deposit. The broker, however, can change this and the interest rate at any time.

-An Example of an Actual Margin Trade

A trader deposits $5,000 into an empty margin account. The broker or brokerage platform has a 40% maintenance requirement and charges 5% interest on loans under $20,000.

The investor purchases a public share of company X. In a normal trading account, he can only purchase stocks worth $5,000. In contrast, the investor can invest $9,000 on company X's stocks. At $10 per share, he can buy 900 shares.

But, what if the stock's value fell? The trader will still have to repay $9,000. This is the amount he borrowed through the margin loan.

-The Risks in Margin Trading

All investors and traders must consider the risks that come with trading securities on margin. The risks include the following:

> Brokerage firms can increase interest rates and margin requirements at anytime

> Failure to avoid losses can result in bankruptcy

> You can lose more money than you have invested. And, you're legally responsible for paying outstanding debts.

> When the value of the security purchased on margin declines, you will need additional funds to pay off your debt.

> They can do it without your notice.

> Usually, there's no time extension for new investors.

> Under the law, the brokerage platform can sell your securities if the account equity falls below the maintenance requirement.

> A short position can cost you. Often, when a stock is halted or delisted stocks, you may still need to pay for interest.

> When the price of an asset takes too long to recover, the debt will result in high-interest costs.

> Investors often add funds to their accounts to maintain maintenance requirements.

Margin trading can amplify your financial portfolio. It increases both the profit and loss potential of your capital. But ultimately, margin trading can increase the chances of generating more profits.

The Different Types of Forex Trades

1) Spot trades

Spot contract or spot trading is the most common type of Forex trade. It's quick and simple. Now, what exactly is it? A Forex spot transaction is also known as an FX spot. It's basically an agreement between two market participants to purchase one currency against another at a predetermined price for settlement on a spot date.

An FX spot is a bilateral agreement. This means that two parties are involved in one transaction. The contract is considered an agreement. It's a binding obligation to sell or buy a determined amount of a foreign currency at a spot exchange rate. This is the predetermined price that you must pay on the spot date. Simply put, an FX spot is a binding obligation to buy/sell a specific amount of foreign currency.

2) Forward contracts

Forward contracts can protect you against market volatility. What's so bad about market volatility? Volatility, which is defined as the statistical measure of the price fluctuation of an asset, increases risks and makes it hard for beginner traders to gain profits.

The value of assets can change over time. If a particular currency experiences daily fluctuations, then you can say that it's volatile. By small or large amounts, the prices of assets, including stocks, futures, and currencies, can decrease or increase. The term "market volatility" describes the range of the changes in an asset's price.

For example, if the value of a stock remains consistent for a long time, then it has low volatility. The same can be said when its price experiences minimal price movement. Generally, high volatility makes a trade or investment risky. It also spells great potential for losses or gains.

3) Window forward

A window forward trade is a forward contract. However, the settlement in this transaction isn't predetermined. And, it has two agreed dates for future transactions. You can benefit from this type of contract if you desire to secure a currency exchange rate. This allows you to meet a commitment with a flexible date.

Once you know the settlement date, you can settle the contract within the window. If you fail to settle your account within the timeframe, you can settle the contract but the exchange rate may be modified. You, as the trader, may be required to provide a margin or deposit. This happens if the payment has been overdue.

4) Limit order

A limit order, in contrast to an FX spot, is a type of Forex order to trade a stock at a specific price. Two types of this trade exist: buy limit and sell limit. You can execute a buy limit at the predetermined price or lower. On the other hand, you can only carry out a sell limit order. If the asset's market value reaches the limit price, you can fill a limit order.

5) Stop Loss Order

A stop\loss order specifies that an asset is sold or bought when it reaches the stop price. This is the specific price in a stop order. It generates a market order--an order to buy or sell a security immediately. A market order doesn't guarantee the execution price, but it does ensure the execution of the order.

When the stop price is met, the stop order serves as a market order. It is then executed at the soonest available opportunity. Often, a stop/loss order is utilized to avoid losses when the value of an asset drops. You can send an order to brokers if your investment starts to look risky.

Also, with a stop/loss order, you're instructed to purchase if the exchange rate becomes lower than the stop price. Many traders combine a stop/loss and limit order. Doing so protects them from a sudden decrease in the rates.

Aside from making profits, preserving and managing your capital should be your most important task as a trader. Once you lose your trading capital, it will be hard earning back what you've lost.

Every day poses new challenges in trading. Global politics, economic events, and central bank news can affect currency prices, either positively or negatively.

The Risks in Trading Forex

Like other financial markets, the Forex market also has risks that you need to take note of, and they can greatly affect the success of your currency trades.

1) Interest rate risk

Fluctuations in interest rates can impact exchange rates. When the interest rate rises, the foreign exchange rate of a currency increases as well.

A low volatile currency attracts foreign investors. This, in turn, strengthens the value of that currency, making it more stable than before and highly sought after in financial markets.

When the value of the currency weakens, the interest rate decreases too. Interest rates, alone, can cause fluctuations in a domestic currency's value.

-How to mitigate the effects of interest rate risk?

- ➢ Holding bonds of multiple durations

- ➢ Hedging fixed income with swaps, options, or derivatives

- ➢ Purchasing of high-yield or floating-rate currency pairs

    2) Counterparty risk

In FX markets, the counterparty is the platform or entity where you close and open positions. Simply put, a counterparty could be a broker or a dealer.

Counterparty risks encompass platform defaults and broker loopholes. It's defined as the "probability that the other party in a trade may not carry out its part of the deal and neglect contractual obligations.

You should choose a well-reputed and well-established counterparty. It must boast authentic reviews that come from genuine and real people, not from bots or paid reviewers.

You should also care to check the age of the brokerage company and the number of its MAU, or monthly active users.

3) Country risk

The economic and political status of the issuing country can affect the exchange rate of a domestic currency.

This risk refers to the uncertainty that is associated with trading a currency being issued by a country that has a lot of political turmoil or is economically unstable.

It can arise because of any of the factors below:

- ➢ Exchange-rate

- ➢ Economic news and events

- ➢ Political instability

- ➢ Exchange rate

- ➢ Technological influences

-How to mitigate country risk?

- ➢ Time your investments wisely

- ➢ Borrow domestically

- ➢ Consider devaluation risks when trading exotic and minor pairs

- ➢ Diverse, disperse, and exit

- ➢ Spreading of buy price if there's an impending devaluation

    4) Liquidity risk

Liquidity risk is considered a financial risk. For a specific period, a given security or financial asset cannot be traded as swiftly enough without impacting the market price.

At times, a currency pair or any financial instrument can't be sold due to a lack of liquidity. This can arise from any of the following:

> Lengthening of the holding period for VaR calculations

> Creating explicit liquidity reserves

> Widening of spreads

-How to mitigate liquidity risks

> Create a contingency plan

> Conduct regular stress test

> Control and monitor liquidity daily

> Make an effort to identify risks early

5) Transaction risk

The time gap between the closing and opening of a transaction creates possible risks. This refers to the negative effect that FX rate fluctuations can have on a completed transaction before settlement. It's actually the currency or rate of exchange risk associated with the time delay between entering and exiting a trade.

-The factors that contribute to transaction risks

> Errors in handling and communication

- ➢ Price fluctuations

- ➢ Long time differential between initiation and settlement

- ➢ Volatility

- ➢ Bull and bear markets

-The best strategies to mitigate currency risks

- ➢ Hedging with ETFs

- ➢ Reducing credit and market risks

- ➢ Engaging in currency swaps, an FX swap involves trading interest and principal in one currency for another

- ➢ Purchase of forward contracts

- ➢ Trading only home currencies

- ➢ Risk sharing, which involves sharing of exposure risk with mutual understanding

The Best Time Frame for Your Forex Trades

Beginner traders often trade in the wrong time frame. You, as a newbie FX trader, must base your trading time on your capital, availability, and personality.

What's the importance of time-frames in Forex trading? Time frames play critical roles in developing an effective trading system. If you prefer a wide investment, using multiple time frames must be included in your strategy.

As a rule of thumb, three-time frames can be sufficient to give you a detailed and broad market reading of your target currency pair. Lesser than three-time frames leave openings for trading risks. Your trading strategy shall determine the duration for each frame.

Most swing traders have little use for hours or minutes in duration since they often take positions that last for months. The opposite is true for day traders because they tend to cut losses by closing positions before the end of every trading day.

Highly successful traders know how to use time frames to support their trading styles. Day trading in foreign exchanges can be both advantageous and profitable since it's a very volatile market. Hence, the use of multiple time frames is beneficial to day traders.

The use of various FX time frames can help you spot large trades and regular price actions that are still unfolding. You can form different viewpoints while switching between two or more time frames on the same currency pair.

-What are the Major FX Time Frames?

What are they? They're short-term, medium-term, and long-term. You have the option of using all three. Others use one short and one long when considering potential trades. Long time frames are beneficial in determining trade set-ups. In contrast, short time frames can help in timing market entries.

Short-term time frames are used by scalpers and day traders. The trend is usually hourly or 4-hour, but some opt for a minute duration. Trigger time frames usually last for 15 minutes.

Because of the volatility of the currency market, FX day traders chose short terms. In doing so, they can observe meaningful data. Medium-term for an illiquid asset may not provide any valuable data points.

Due to the nature of the Forex Market, switching between various time frames during different sessions (e.g. US, Asian, European) generates various market conditions.

These are system and business-related issues that you can use for determining indicators. You can use such indicators to look for trends specific to US, Asia, or European sessions.

-What's a trading session?

A trading session is a period matching the daytime trading for the trading hours in a given region. In general, it's a 24-hour business day in the financial market. The duration between the opening bell and the closing bell is the trading session.

Key Takeaways:

> Primary trading hours differ from one country to another. They're dependent on the time zones.

> A trading session is the major trading hours for a particular locale or asset.

> The sessions vary by country and asset class. For US stocks, the regular trading session starts at 9:30 and closes at 16:00. For the US bond market, the regular weekday trading session starts at 8:00 and ends at 17:00. It closes at 14:00 on six occasions and is unavailable on 10 holidays.

> ➢ Traders must be aware of the different trading hours for any security that they want to trade.

-What FX Time Frame Should You Choose?

To choose the most optimal time frame for your trades, take into consideration your strategy and trading style. These should be the factors that greatly influence your preferred time frame. Hence, choose a chart that you're comfortable with and execute a very thorough analysis. Also, make sure to establish risk management on your trades.

Day trading forex can be difficult. Beginner traders using a speculating strategy expose themselves to trading decisions that haven't been tested and proven effective for very long. This deadly combination of frequency and experience paves the way for losses that could be prevented by a different approach like position trading.

Scalpers, as well as day traders, should, at all times, specialize in minuscule price actions. This is why you could trade with just 5-minute or 10-minute time frames. They tend to move quickly in the direction of the price. With this, they are tied to the charts and the trends.

That's what day traders who take hourly positions do. In contrast, those who take a shorter-term approach have a smaller margin of error than its opposite type.

Day traders can evaluate trends on hourly charts and find possible price points. This refers to a point on a graph of possible prices. From given points, some could generate profits.

Entry opportunities are abundant in "minute" time frames like five- or fifteen-minute charts.

Day Trading Forex

Scalpers or day traders need the price of the trading asset to move in favor of their prediction. Hence, they've to practice vigilance when observing charts. Day traders can speculate to evaluate trends on an hourly chart. On minute time frames, like 5-minute charts, they can spot entry points.

An entry point is the price at which a trader sells or buys a security. Usually, it's a component of a specified trading strategy developed for reducing investment risks and removing sentiments from trading decisions. Remember, a good entry point is, oftentimes, a result of a successful trade.

Here are some technical analysis strategies, which you can use to identify any trend:

> The use of 200-day MAs for scalpers utilizing daily and hourly trading time frames

> Identify and understand Forex trendlines

> The use of MACD indicator

A trend line is like a line drawn under pivot lows or pivot thighs to show the current price movement and for predicting future price actions. Trendlines serve as visuals of resistance and support in any trading time frame. They can present the speed and direction of the price and describe patterns in compressions.

Aside from those, you can use the following technical analysis when identifying entry levels, such as the following:

> MA crossovers

> The utilization of key levels of resistance and support

> The use of indicators, including MACD and RSI

> Candlestick analysis

-Day Trading with Multiple Trading Time Frames

Successful Forex day traders, including George Soros and Bill Lipschutz, tend to use multiple time frame analysis. This involves viewing a currency pair at two or more time frames.

Executing Your First Trade

Assuming that you already have a trading account that enables trading forex, all you have to do is to follow the straightforward steps below. Also, don't forget to prepare your trading system for your first-ever currency trade.

1) Launch the Platform

In Chapter 2, you've learned how to choose the right broker for your capital and trading strategy. Once you've installed the platform on your smartphone or personal computer, open the application to launch it. If you chose a web-based platform, then you should sign in to your account on your broker's website.

To finish this step, log in to your trading account by providing your username and password. Now, take caution when you're logging in. You must always secure your account credentials, and remember, it's best to use a trustworthy VPN.

2) Open the Chart

In this step, you've to choose a currency pair. You must open a chart and choose a time frame. For instance, you choose a 20-minute time frame. In this case, each candlestick on the opened chart represents 20 minutes.

3) Add the Indicators

When you've chosen a currency pair, you need to work on your chart and add indicators. You can opt for technical indicators. For example, you may add MACD and a 300 exponential moving average. The basic rule for the use of a 300 EMA is that if the currency's exchange rate is above the line, then it may increase. If the price is below the 300 EMA line, then it may continue going down.

In the 2nd scenario, it's confirmed that the exchange rate is decreasing unstably. The use of technical indicators can be helpful in this step, in the decision-making process.

However, if you're selling the given currency pair, then it means you're buying JPY and selling AUD. Hence, you need to look at the strengths of the quote currency and the weaknesses of the base, which is the Australian dollar. With the MACD, you can look for signs that AUD's value is indeed going down.

When utilized alone, the MACD indicator isn't always reliable. But, if you use it as an element of a complex trading system, it can accurately pinpoint a possible future price.

In case the price is fighting the downtrend, it's advised to wait for the crossing and heading down of the MACD indicators. You should do this before making a trade.

4) Calculating profits

Of course, this is also an essential part of forex trading since it's a very different form of trading from the rest. Here are the key points you need to remember when calculating profits in this market:

➤ A pip is used to measure the difference in value between two domestic currencies. A pip is equivalent to 0.0001 of a change in value. For instance, if your EUR/USD Forex trade moves from 1.645 to 1646, then the currency value has increased by ten pips.

➤ Multiply the pips number that your trading account has by the rate of exchange. The product will tell you how much your trading funds have decreased or increased in value.

5) Place the Order

After studying the charts and rethinking and reconfirming your strategy, preparing to place an order is next. In the example mentioned in the previous section, the price of the currency pair is decreasing, so it's best to go short.

Remember, a short position is a sell position. Traders take this position if they believe that the stock's value will decrease or continue to decrease. If the price indeed drops, you can repurchase the stock at a lower price. By doing so, you can make a profit.

6) Establish the Levels for Stop/Loss and Take Profit

Step 5 is optional, but this step is highly recommended. Setting a stop/loss order at 1/2 pip can lead to long-term success. Why is this so? With such a setup, you're right 50% of the time, and you can still come out of the trade at the end of the day. However, this is only possible if your risk-reward is indeed favorable.

Setting a stop/loss order can limit losses if the market moves in the predicted direction. Establishing a take profit level ensures that you can exit your trade with profit. Setting these two levels when placing the trade can be advantageous. This is because it is difficult to make decisions once the trade is actually in the market.

7) Confirm Your Order

When you have set the necessary levels, it's time to submit an order and wait for confirmation. On-screen, it may appear as a dialogue box. Remember, the "confirmation" is important, as well as the ticket number. In case there's something wrong in the execution phase, you can contact the broker and present your ticket number. Doing this can help your broker correct the mistake and refund credits.

8) The Waiting Period

After order confirmation, the waiting period begins. Many day traders turn off their screen and stay away from the market for some time. Although it's advised to constantly watch the market, you can sit back and relax if you've properly set up your trade, like establishing a take profit or stop loss order before confirmation.

9) Trade Completion

This is the last step in the Forex trading process. With the given example, the trade could've resulted in a take profit.

After this, it's a must to way your losses and profits. Above all, avoid letting your emotions cloud your trading judgments. Just because your winning, don't get carried away by the excitement and start getting careless. You didn't study this book for that.

The foreign exchange market is like the ocean. You'll see a lot of ups and downs and more fluctuations. What matters the most is to continue your analysis of prices, assets, and indicators.

The Law of Supply and Demand

In foreign exchanges, like in floating markets, crowd psychology, as well as the interactions between traders, determine the prices and rates of assets/goods. The buyers in the market represent the demand for a product, security, or commodity.

On the contrary, the sellers and the security they offer represent the supply in the market. If the supply and demand are in balance, the price of the asset in the electronic market will be unchanged for some time.

However, if that becomes imbalanced, then the price of the asset in question will either rise or fall. When demand surpasses supply, the total number of buyers in the market exceeds the number of sellers.

Chapter Summary

Trading Forex on electronic markets or brokerage platforms can be a thrilling hobby and a good source of additional income. To some, profit generation here is slower than stock trading. Still, it offers lower risks since the market is very volatile and highly liquid! Billions of trades are executed per day in Forex marketplaces all over the world. Now that you know all the risks, processes, terminologies, and technicalities in Forex, it's time to execute your first Forex trade.

Step 7: Day Trading Futures and Cryptocurrencies

You've learned how to conduct technical and fundamental analysis, as well as read charts, indicators, and balance sheets. You now know the many ways for day trading Forex and stocks. But, how about the other remaining securities that are also profitable these days? This chapter is all about them. You will finally meet "futures" and "cryptocurrencies."

While employing various strategies and techniques to capitalize on perceived market inefficiencies, day traders take maximum advantage of the fluctuations in the market. They are prevalent in the markets where price actions of securities are volatile and frequent.

Whether you want to supplement your other day trading endeavors or you just prefer straightforward financial securities, you can learn how to make money from other tradable assets, in this chapter.

Cryptocurrency Day Trading: Making $100 per Day

In recent years, crypto trading has boomed. The high trading volume and volatility of the most popular cryptocurrencies (e.g, bitcoin and ethereum) perfectly suit speculators, like day traders.

The rise of bitcoin and other cryptocurrencies has made the market what it is today--a highly volatile electronic market. Remember, volatility and liquidity are what successful speculators, like Warren Buffet and Tim Sykes, highly sought after.

However, you must choose the right coin. As of writing, there are over 1,600 crypto coins out there. Not all of them can give you profit. Yes, millions of trades occur in this market, but they only involve the most popular cryptocurrencies.

The crypto market provides many opportunities for speculators if they do trades right. This section presents a step-by-step guide for the most lucrative type of electronic trading: crypto trading.

Here are the things you need to do to get started:

1. Choose coins that are highly liquid and volatile

Today, bitcoin is the most traded cryptocurrency. Hence, bitcoin is your best choice. The demand for this crypto coin is very high. In February 2021, the price of 1 BTC spiked to

In just a month, its value has increased to $20,000, from $32,000 in January 15, 2021 to $5,000 by February 18, 2021.

Bitcoin's value is very volatile. What's more, the best part about it is that its price has retained an upward trend in the past years. A sudden significant downtrend will unlikely happen in the coming months.

Ripple, Ethereum, and Litecoin are among the best bitcoin alternatives. You may also opt to day trade minor and exotic coins. However, unlike bitcoin and its alternatives, the price of such crypto coins can plummet as fast as they've risen.

For the full list, please refer below:

-The major cryptocurrencies

> Bitcoin

> Litecoin

> Ethereum

> Zcash

> Stellar Lumen

> Cardano

- ➢ Polkadot

- ➢ Stellar

- ➢ Chainlink

- ➢ Binance coin

- ➢ Tether

- ➢ Monero

2. Apply the money flow index (MFI) indicator on a 5-minute chart

The Money Flow Index indicator is a simple technical indicator. This is utilized to monitor the price movement of e-coins and to gauge when will noteworthy organizations start trading a specific cryptocurrency.

The settings for this indicator should be set at three periods. The default levels for buying and selling must be between the range of 80 to 100 and 20 to 0, respectively. You can learn how to use this indicator in the next step.

3. Use the MFI indicator

A value near 100 indicates the presence of large entities in the market. When big sharks make purchases, they can't hide their digital tracks. They leave evidence of their market activities. The MFI indicator is employed when reading their activities.

To further increase the accuracy of readings and predictions, day traders skip the first two readings even if the result is 100. They do this to fine-tune their strategies and study the reactions of the crypto price. The price must hold up during the 1st and 2nd MFI readings with a value of 100.

If the value of the cryptocurrency is below 100 after the first two readings, then the price may go down throughout the rest of that day. Now, it's time to determine the right marketplace where you can trade cryptocurrencies and satisfy the technical conditions required.

4. Taking a buy position

The subsequent 100 MFI readings present ripe opportunities to make profitable trades. As long as the technical conditions are met, you can treat that result as the right indication.

However, except for the 100 MFI reading, the candlestick needs to be bullish. A candlestick is a price chart displaying the low, high, and open closing prices of a financial security for a given period. The close must be near the upper and its wicks should be small.

When all of that has been taken into account, you need to establish protective stop-loss orders and determine where you can make profits. For this, please refer to the next step.

5. Make your purchase

Eugene Loza (EXCAVO) said, "It's best for crypto day traders to hide their protective stop/loss below the day's low and take profit in the first 60 minutes after opening a trade."

A break below the day's low indicates an impending shift in market sentiment or a reversal day. In such cases, you should get out of the market as soon as possible.

A break can occur as a swift price increase or decrease or as a gap, in which trading transpires at multiple prices along the way. A breakout can occur when the value of the asset breaks above the resistance level or drops below the support level.

In day trading cryptocurrencies, the rule of thumb is to take profit during the 1st hour after you finally make a trade. There's a low success rate in holding trades longer.

Advanced Tips for Crypto Trading

To earn a high return, you must take risks. That's a fact in the electronic trading world. When making money in the short-term, you need to greatly consider the market's volatility.

Like in other markets, the prices of the major cryptocurrencies on charts are composed of different types of trends, including mini trends. With FA and TA, you can study the trends to make value predictions.

Short-term trading is also sub-divided into a few different categories. They're based on how quickly you realize days, hours, or weeks.

Crypto day trading is an aggressive form of short-term trading. Your goal as the trader is to sell coins within the trading day and make a profit before going to bed.

In conventional electronic exchanges, a trading day ends at 4:30 pm. The crypto market, however, runs 24/7. Let's start with learning the different crypto trading sessions.

-Defining the crypto trading sessions

Since crypto coins can be traded internationally, disregarding borders, you can opt for the trading sessions of Tokyo, New York, Australia, and the Eurozone. They're considered the financial capitals of the world.

They're quite similar to the sessions in the FX market. Some sessions might provide better opportunities if the coin you plan to trade has a higher volume in that time frame than in others. For example, NEO, a cryptocurrency that is based in China, oftentimes experience its highest trading volume during the Asian session.

The prospect of having the ability to trade night or day can be beneficial for you. Whether you're experiencing a sleepless night or you're having a lunch break, you can just open your trading app or web-based broker and start trading. However, remember that even though you have this flexibility, you mustn't neglect the fundamentals. Always conduct a thorough analysis of the market.

-Secure your crypto wallet

A crypto wallet can either be a device, service, program, or physical medium that allows for the storage of public or private keys. The keys are utilized for cryptocurrency trades and offer data encryption. This is perhaps the most well-known and most valued feature of crypto wallets. A simple crypto wallet can be utilized to receive/spend cryptocurrencies, track ownership, and store digital coins, like BTCs and NEOs.

Contrary to simple wallets that only require one party for transaction confirmation, multi-signature wallets need two or more parties to execute a trade. That's why they're more secured than simple crypto wallets. In the digital currency space. The signing keys for smart contracts are also stored in wallets

-Choosing a crypto wallet

In choosing a digital wallet for your crypto coins, you must consider the people who will have access to your private keys. Remember, those people will be signing capabilities. This means they can access your wallet any time of the day. If you opt for a third-party provider, you have to place your trust in the entity in keeping your coins safe.

In the case of the Mt. Gox exchange scandal, most of their clients lost BTCs. On March 9, 2014, the firm filed for bankruptcy. Many claimed that that bitcoin exchanged is fraudulent. Please keep in mind that downloading a wallet doesn't guarantee that you're the only one who can access it.

For getting started, here are some tips for choosing a secured crypto wallet:

- ➤ Multi-currency enabled

- ➤ Accessible and user-friendly

- ➤ Can be accessed offline

- ➤ It comes from a well-refuted provider with good reviews

- ➤ Enhanced security

- ➤ The provider is licensed and regulated and has been around for at least six years

For receiving digital options, you don't need a key for the receiving wallet. You or the sending party just need the destination address. Anyone can send crypto coins to the address. Only the individual or entity who has access to the private key of the corresponding address can utilize the address.

If you're day trading in the crypto market, make sure that you aren't paying for a lot of service and commission fees. Before you engage in any actual short-term trading, consult your broker first and check if their regulations and fees coincide with your trading strategy. Ask yourself, "Can I generate profit in this platform with my trading capital?"

Here's a simple step-by-step strategy you can use for day trading crypto coins:

1) With technical analysis, confirm the existence and the future direction of the trend.

2) Anticipate for a pullback.

3) Purchase at the pullback during an uptrend. To do this, closely watch for mini trends.

4) Take profit at the resistance level. Crypto day trading can be a lucrative business because of the market's high volatility.

Remember, high volatility and liquidity suit day traders very well. Crypto trading could be the environment where you can succeed. If you feel like you aren't into this type of day trading, then do check out the following sections for futures and options.

Everything You Need to Know About Day Trading Futures

What's a future? A futures contract is an agreement to trade a commodity or financial security at a predetermined price and set date.

Major online brokers feature a trading section for futures. You must familiarize yourself with their rules and requirements first before finally choosing any of them.

Investors consider futures trading as a method to broaden their portfolio and maximize profits. Day traders trade futures to earn both instant and gradual income.

-Futures vs. Options

Futures contracts for stocks, bonds, and market indices exist, and they can be considered as cash-settled contracts.

Options contracts, on the other hand, provide traders the right but not the obligation to buy a security. The owner of a call option can buy a given asset at a specific value for a given period. However, the holder of the security has no obligation to purchase the asset.

With a futures contract, both the seller and buyer of the contract are required to transact at a predetermined date and time. In day trading, the trade is often executed the same day that the contract is bought.

Futures also require a daily settling of losses and gains. This means traders must balance their trading accounts when every trading day ends. This may seem like an inconvenience, but depending on the market's flow, you may need to deposit more funds in your trading account until the contract is fulfilled.

With options trading, there are no such daily additions. In the next section, transacting in the options market is further discussed.

-How are Futures Regulated?

Because of the rise of futures trading, tight regulations were established. The regulations ensure that all parties involved in every futures trade are secured. One example is the Commodity Exchange Act, which was passed by the US Congress in 1936. Although the rules have evolved over the years, the framework of the act has remained intact.

In 1974, the Commodity Futures Trading Commission (CFTC) was formed. Five committees comprise the CFTC. The US president appoints the commissioners; they serve 5-year terms and are responsible for setting price fluctuations. The US government regulates futures trading on brokers that are registered in the USA.

Like options and stock traders, futures traders can also use leveraging and margin trading. However, these are dependent on their broker or the platform they're in.

In terms of trading futures, you have to be vigilant, like in any markets. Futures are often traded during after hours and outside traditional trading hours. With this, when the market reopens, you'll have a good idea of the status of the asset due to the overnight changes evident on your chart.

-Where to trade

Major online brokers have a trading section specially dedicated to this financial instrument. Before choosing a broker and settling for it, you must familiarize yourself with their rules and requirements.

In terms of margin trading futures, brokers only provide a margin account to users they certify that can pay back the loan and interest. Accessibility to margin usually requires a specific amount of funds in your original trading account.

Some brokers, like TD Ameritrade, require passing a test or class before one can begin margin trading. TradeStation, Interactive Brokers, and TD Ameritrade are some brokerage platforms that allow for margin trading futures.

-The risks in futures trading

Ben Fitzsimmons, an algorithmic trader, says, "Unlike stocks and equities, futures don't pay dividends or provide incentives that investors can gain over time." Futures are quite different from other financial instruments. They're a 100% zero-sum game. When one trader losses, another one makes a profit.

Barry Johnson, one of the UK's top financial analysts and equities trader, says, "The futures market doesn't represent any ownership to anything." Futures are just side bets and have no economic value. Nevertheless, each part of a trade pays commissions and other service costs.

Nevertheless, futures trading paves the way for traders to hedge investments and engage in daily scalping.

-Choosing a future

Once you've selected a broker and have set up your trading account, you must then choose a futures contract. For this step, you've to consider several factors, including the indicators below:

> Volume

Choose contracts that have a trading volume of 300,000 trades per day. Doing this allows you to trade on the levels you want. And, due to such liquidity, another trader will always want to take your offer as long as it's reasonable. A few of the most traded contracts are listed below:

a) Crude oil WTI

b) 10-year treasury note

c) GE or Eurodollar

d) ES or E-mini S&P 500

Once you've selected a profitable futures contract, you must next consider its price movements and the margins that fit your style of trading. The available margin depends on the amount and agreements your broker offers. For example, margin trading of crude oil contracts often demands high account deposits.

> Movement

To establish price movement, you need to consider two factors. The first one is point value and the number of points the contract moves within 24 hours. By calculating the simple average true range (ATR), you can get the data you need to enter a profitable position in this market.

For the formula, please refer to the image below:

$$TR = \text{Max}[(H - L), \text{Abs}(H - C_P), \text{Abs}(L - C_P)]$$

$$ATR = \left(\frac{1}{n}\right) \sum_{(i=1)}^{(n)} TR_i$$

where:

TR_i = A particular true range

n = The time period employed

To calculate the range, look at the difference between the low and the high prices of the future in the present day. Remember, "true high" is yesterday's close and today's high. "True low" represents yesterday's close and today's low. Meanwhile, "true range" refers to the true high less the true low.

To better understand this concept, take the following scenario as an example. If the future closes in the day at ninety, then gaps will open at ninety-one and may reach an intraday high at ninety-two. In this case, the true range is 90 to 92 since yesterday's close is at 90 and the true high is 92.

-Using the factors and indicators

Today, you can confidently choose the type of futures contract to trade especially that you now know how to read the market. Will you choose equities contracts related to commodities or crude oil?

The E-Mini futures is a good starting point for beginner day traders. You can avail of margins that are as low as $600. This futures market is more volatile than that of crude oil's. With the E-Mini S&P 500, you can start trading with just a $3,000 trading account.

Conclusion

The journey has been long, hasn't it? There have been ups and downs, like the fluctuations on price charts. Trends are there, and like a startup business, you need to watch their performance. Will the price continue to go up? Will the trends experience a sudden reversal? TA and FA are your go-to tools for analyzing the trends and the factors that affect price movement.

Indicators, such as the EPS, volume, and P/E ratio, are the main ingredients for technical and fundamental analysis. Even the classic strategy "buy low and sell high" strategy makes use of such indicators. After that, you need to determine support and resistance levels to come up with profitable trading plans.

Once you have all the elements in place, you need to set up orders and parameters for your trades. If you can't watch the markets that closely, consider using a stop/loss order. In doing so, even if the price of the security keeps decreasing, you can get out of the market before it hits all-time bottom. In their respective chapters, all of these methods, techniques, and strategies have been covered.

Day trading is all about dealing with volatile assets. As a day trader, you won't profit from stagnation. You can only increase your savings and capital if you buy/sell financial instruments that exhibit price fluctuations. Your profit will depend on the success of your trades and how you efficiently read indicators and market sentiment. There's no shortcut to day trading. It's a step-by-step process, but by following the teachings in this book, you can start making a profit from tradable securities and grow your wealth every day.